The Anatomy
of the
Body of God

> Being
> The Supreme Revelation
> of Cosmic Consciousness

EXPLAINED AND DEPICTED IN GRAPHIC FORM BY

Frater Achad

WITH DESIGNS SHOWING THE

FORMATION, MULTIPLICATION, AND PROJECTION

OF

THE STONE OF THE WISE

BY

Will Ransom

ISBN 1-56459-140-9

UNITY SCHOOL LIBRARY
UNITY VILLAGE, MISSOURI 64065

Request our FREE CATALOG of Hundreds of
Rare Esoteric Books
Unavailable Elsewhere

Alchemy, Ancient Wisdom, Astronomy, Baconian, Eastern-Thought, Egyptology, Esoteric, Freemasonry, Gnosticism, Hermetic, Magic, Metaphysics, Mysticism, Mystery Schools, Mythology, Occult, Philosophy, Psychology, Pyramids, Qabalah, Religions, Rosicrucian, Science, Spiritual, Symbolism, Tarot, Theosophy, *and many more!*

Kessinger Publishing Company
P.O. Box 160-C, Kila, MT 59920
(406) 756-0167

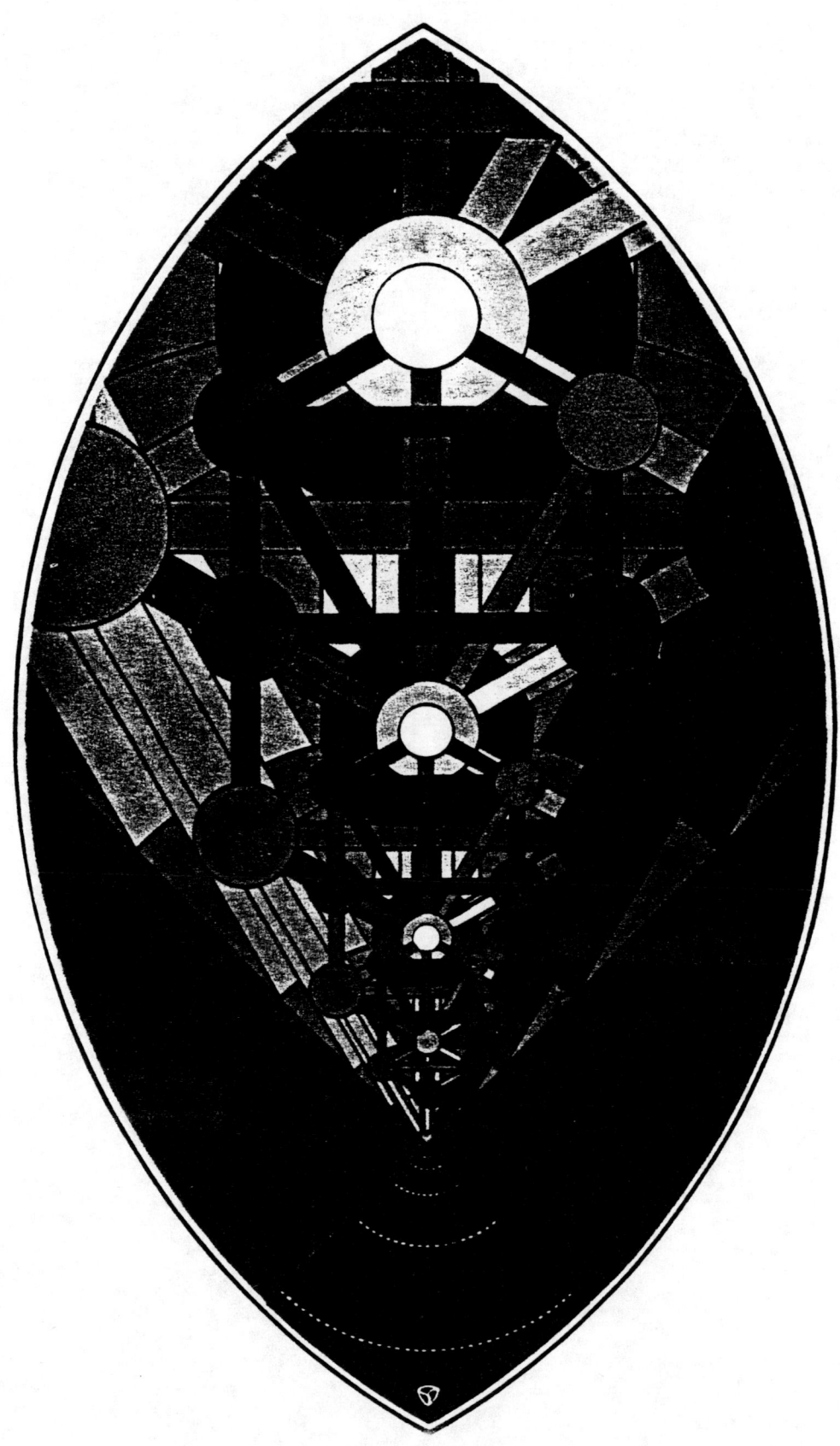

PREFACE

Although the title of this short essay may seem, to some who have not read its contents, to be both presumptuous and unwarrantable, it is hoped that these will reserve their judgment until they have given due attention and consideration to the study of such an important subject.

We are living in strange times. Civilization seems rapidly to be breaking up, while yet some inner urge is at work towards a better and more balanced construction in many departments of life.

One of the results of the Great War has been to turn the minds of many people from some of the narrower conceptions of life into wider channels. A spirit of enquiry has become apparent on the part of those who had previously been content to accept statements in regard to life's deeper issues on mere belief or hearsay. Many new Movements have arisen under the guidance of people who have obtained at least a partial glimpse of man's wider heritage, and there has been a corresponding falling away from what may be termed the orthodox or established order of things in the churches and elsewhere. Many countries have been making experiments of various kinds, most of which, however, being the outcome of "reform movements" of the narrowest sort, are quickly proving themselves to be unsatisfactory and inadequate. At present, amid all these indications, there seems to have been no complete solution in sight, and, so it might appear, very little comprehension, even on the part of those who are honestly doing their best under the circumstances, of the underlying principles involved. Those who should really be in a position to help, are unable to do so effectively for the same reason.

It may seem a far cry from the present world-conditions of a social and political nature to the Holy Qabalah, but help sometimes comes from quite unexpected sources.

The Jews, and the Jewish problem, represent very important aspects of the difficulty and its solution. A great proportion of the wealth of the world is today in the hands of the Jews, yet as a nation they have no place. As the "chosen people" they were an important nation, but the rejection of the Teacher in whom they expected to find their Messiah, is usually considered to have been the cause of their becoming wanderers upon the face of the Earth. Yet the word "Jew" is derived from IU, the Ever-Coming Son, the Horus of the earliest Egyptian traditions, whose influence is not confined to the Christian Era but extends to all Ages, and of Whom all truly typical God-Men, such as Jesus, have been, and are, the representatives upon earth.

But the Jews have neglected the study of their own "Chokmah Nestorah," or Secret Wisdom Tradition, as transmitted in the Holy Qabalah, thus losing sight of their True Will as a nation and their essential Purpose in the Great Creative Plan. It has remained for the Gentile to rediscover some of the deeper mysteries of this Ancient Wisdom, and these are found to be the same in essence as those of Catholicism, Freemasonry, Pythagorean Philosophy, Hermetism, and so forth; in fact there has always been a Universal Tradition which when known has led the Nations to the height of civilization, and when lost has heralded their decline and downfall.

The present world-crisis and breaking up of civilization is due to the necessity of a general "clean-up" preparatory to a wider and grander conception being presented to humanity than has been possible for many thousands of years. All thinking people realize that things are in a critical condition, and all should be prepared to grasp any reasonable opportunity of obtaining a solution which will be of permanent, rather than temporary value.

Things cannot be put right without effort, and the question arises: "In what direction is effort most necessary?"

The solution lies with the individual; it is useless to talk of reforming others until we have reformed ourselves. It is equally useless to rely upon someone else to do for us what we are quite capable of doing and should do for ourselves. The soul of Man—which is the plastic mediator between body and spirit—has become distorted; he must learn to rectify its structure before he can obtain a clear outlook and a proper point of view.

Man's teachers have been largely responsible for distorting his mental vision, and they must cease from restricting his natural actions and impeding his natural growth, which would be normally proportioned if the Holy Spirit within him were allowed to expand in the proper manner. Man's natural tendency is towards health of body and soul under the action of Spirit. Most of the present systems have led him to believe otherwise from his earliest childhood, thus handicapping him from the start.

The child is, in one sense, the best example of the perfect man or woman, and if the child were allowed to develop Intelligence unhampered by false notions from outside, it would grow to be the true example of the God-Man or Man-God in the majority of cases. We have ruined our children before they have had a chance to come to maturity; our well-meaning, though ignorant, parents and childhood teachers have instilled into our subconscious minds most of the "complexes" which in after life we can only eradicate by bitter toil and bloody sweat.

Yet I thank God for a good mother, whose simple faith, transmitted to me, has given me the quiet courage and perseverance to unravel some, at least, of those ignorantly transmitted "knots" and kinks. But, for all that, humanity *has* complexes which need to be unraveled and straightened out before much real work can be done.

First, then, let me make an appeal on behalf of the children, even if in this New Aeon they do not so much need my support since they are showing an independence of spirit which is simply astonishing to their parents and guardians who were born and brought up under the Old Dispensation. I make my appeal to these same parents, not to foolishly try to break the Will of the child, for it is God's Will therein, and the only indication of the right course of action. Once this True Will is distorted, and the lower personal will brought out of alignment with it, the city is, so to speak, divided against itself and cannot stand. It is the interior conflict between the "personal" and the "True" Will in each of us, that is the cause of all suffering and all wrong action. There is but one remedy, discover the True Will and then DO IT, and our course is one with Destiny and the Will of the Universe in our regard.

The age of "mothering" children is past. The women of today, failing to do so in regard to their offspring, or having no offspring to "mother" are doing all they can to "mother" the nation, particularly in America. Such "reforms" as Prohibition are largely due to this mistaken zeal for the good of others. What the "Mothers" need most is to learn to mind their own business and to correct their own distorted vision. Repression can never take the place of RIGHT USE on any plane. The Righteous are those who use rightly what they have, for their own good and that of Humanity from which then can never really cut themselves off. Man cannot live, or die, to himself alone. The same is true of Nations.

All things come from One Substance, and are actuated by One Spirit. Rightly used, any aspect of that substance may be taken into the body and soul of Man, and there transmuted into just the proper condition and proportions for the building up of his own particular being.

If, for instance, it were possible to eliminate the effects of wine from all the American people for two or three generations, they would go to the most terrible extremes and act as savages do whose systems have not been used to alcohol, as soon as the habit was revived, as it inevitably would be in the long run. As it is, insofar as their parents have been accustomed to the use of wine, they are comparatively immune while their normal appetites in this respect are not over-stimulated by the attempt at repression. Many of the most normal people drink more under "prohibition" than they ever thought of doing before.

The best men and women are those of such varied experience on all planes that they are immune from every poison and every disease because they have found the proper proportion and balance of all that is called good and evil makes up the Perfect Man who is like unto his Father in Heaven, in Whom all things have their being.

Man must eat of the Tree of the Knowledge of Good and Evil before he comes to the Tree of Life in the midst of the Garden. Only when he eats too much of one thing and not enough of another, does his body or soul become distorted. Every "Christ" and every Genius has been the friend of publicans and sinners, as well as of the "select and exclusive." Idealism and Materialism must unite and go hand in hand if a new Civilization is to be built up. The

Soul of Humanity is the connecting link. There is nothing to be ashamed of in our material bodies, but they would not be of much use without the Spirit and Will which give them Life and motion. On the other hand we should not be so cowardly and selfish as to desire to be re-absorbed into Spirit, as if the whole Creative Plan were a waste of time, and had better never have been started. No! Let us give thanks in our souls for both body and spirit, using both rightly and to the full extent of our power.

But how shall we learn the right proportions of each?

We must eat of the Fruit of the Tree of Life, and it will be found to nourish us perfectly and cause all the elements of our system to come to their proper proportion and fullness of stature. We must learn to overcome the illusions of time and circumstance; we must enter upon the heritage of Freedom that has been prepared for us in the Father's Kingdom upon Earth.

We have sacrificed the flower of Humanity, not alone in the Great War but in many, many ways, to our false gods. In the Name of the True and Living God, let us cease from bloody sacrifice, and start to build a "Living Temple, not made with hands, eternal in the Heavens"—upon Earth.

FRATER ACHAD
Collegium ad Spiritum Sanctum
Box 141, Chicago, Illinois

INTRODUCTION

On April the fourteenth, nineteen hundred and twenty-three E.V., having just completed the ms. of my treatise on "The Egyptian Revival" or The Ever-Coming Son, in which my endeavour was to show that the "Restored Order" of the Paths of the Qabalistic Tree of Life was likely to be the correct one, since it indicated the Universal Tradition as symbolized by the Keys of Hermes, I was rewarded by the opening up of an amazing further possibility in regard to the Design of "The Tree of Life" itself.

It was between 8:30 and 9:30 P.M. on the above date, that the "Tree" began to GROW, and proved itself, to my mind, to be the veritable anatomy of Ra-Hoor-Khuit, Ever-coming, between the two Infinites.

This fresh revelation left me strangely silent; it seemed almost too wonderful to be true, but it has since—for I am writing this on April 17th—shown even greater possibilities, the most extraordinary of which was only revealed to me this afternoon, after discussing the matter with W. R.

I do not intend to write of the discovery itself for the moment, but merely to prepare a brief essay on the Qabalah by means of the further Light I have so recently received. This will serve as an introduction to the more complete explanation of the whole matter which, in order to be comprehensible to my readers, will require a number of diagrams showing the different stages of its development.

To begin at the beginning. As stated in "Q.B.L.," the Qabalists postulated the AIN or NO-THING as the Zero from which, in a mysterious manner, the Universe arose. Next, they say, the AIN SUPH, or Limitless Space, became the Nature of the AIN, and this conception was followed by that of AIN SUPH AUR or the Limitless Light of Chaos.

It was not until this Limitless Light had concentrated Itself to a Centre that the First Positive Idea arose, and this was called Kether and attributed to the Number One.

From this One there arose in succession the other Numerical Emanations or Sephiroth from Two to Ten, thus completing the decimal scale of Numbers. The Number 10 is said to represent the return of the One to Zero, thus completing the Cycle of Manifestation.

These ideas may be found more fully described in "Q.B.L." and elsewhere, but I now desire to attempt a slightly different presentation, which will be developed in greater detail later on in this book.

The finite mind of man is unable to grasp the Infinite, except in a certain Mystical and Spiritual manner, but by the Light of the Spirit let us do our best to comprehend this great mystery of the Beginning.

Let us accept the term AIN as representing That of which Nothing is known, nor can be known, except through the positive manifestations which arise from It. When we attempt to imagine the AIN SUPH—Limitless Space—our minds tend to rush on and on, only to fall back before the Profundity of the Great Deep; yet we have to admit the possibility of Infinite extension in space. In my opinion this is due to the fact that we are only able to extend the *fine material substance* of the mind to a certain limit, after reaching which there is NOTHING for US unless we succeed in developing fresh Power to drive that limit further back and so to extend the actual substance of our being accordingly.

If Life is the Substance of Light, then Life itself is to be considered as the most subtle substance in our make-up, while it would follow that the more this substance is extended, the greater will be our Illumination, the further our range of vision, and the wider our Sphere of Consciousness.

With these thoughts in mind let us attempt to obtain a more complete Understanding of the Primal Process, which is still "going on" Here and Now.

When the AIN SUPH AUR became *concentrated* upon a Single Centre, it *compressed* the Light into the Substance of Light, which is Life. Or, in other words, the Concentrated Light became an inconceivably powerful Force or Energy in the centre of Kether. This Pure Being, or Living Substance, owing to its reaction from the Invisible Centre, tends to expand towards Infinity. This gives us the idea of the Substance of the Universe *ever expanding*, ever occupying more and more of the Limitless Space of the AIN SUPH, while the Primal Centralizing Urge still continues to contract upon the Infinitely Small, or the AIN.

Kether is then the *junction* of these Two Infinites, but particularly represents the *concentration* of the Light to a Point on its way to the Infinitely Small, while Malkuth, the Tenth Sephira and Sphere of the Elements—which the Qabalists say is one with Kether—is the Substance which is *ever expanding* and, so to speak, gradually FILLING UP THE NOTHINGNESS of the AIN SUPH. So we may consider Kether as the Light and Malkuth as the Substance, while the complete Sphere is composed of LIVING SUBSTANCE. This represents the Macrocosmic Universe, but it is ever BECOMING GREATER and GREATER in extent, and driving back, so to speak, the Nothingness of Chaos.

Man, being made in the Image and Likeness of God and of the Universe, has the same infinite possibilities of growth in Consciousness, as the Force of the Spirit extends the substance of his mind to wider and wider fields of thought.

Yet the whole existing Universe is the result of the One Thought of God, and it progresses according to the Order of Pure Reason, as indicated in the Qabalah.

All the Sephiroth and Paths have their place according to this Order, *within* the Sphere of the One Substance, and represent the manifold possibilities of the action of the Life Force upon that Substance and the different manifestations of that Substance under the Influence of the Life Force.

In other words, WITHOUT the manifested universe is the Infinite Body of Nuit; at the CENTRE of All is the Infinitely Small and unextended Essence of Life, or Hadit. The Contraction of Nuit upon Hadit and the Expansion of Hadit into Nuit are constant forces. The Finite Universe, or Ra-Hoor-Khuit, the Ever-Coming Son, is bounded by an EVER WIDENING CIRCUMFERENCE which is always exactly BETWEEN the Infinitely Great and the Infinitely Small.

Kether and Malkuth—Spirit and Matter—together represent this Universal Sphere, while Tiphereth, the Central Sphere of the Tree of Life, must always correspond to Ra-Hoor-Khuit within them; a Sphere HALF-WAY between the Centre and the Circumference.

In Nature we may consider the finite representatives of these two Infinites to be the smallest known atom of matter as the Centre, the widest expanse of the Star Universe as the circumference, and the Central Sun as their child.

In Man we find all these possibilities, both infinite and finite. The true Centre of his being is Hadit whose representative is the tiny Spark of Pure Spiritual Light; the substance of his Mental Body is only limited by the Bounds of the Universe, and these ever recede towards Infinity. His physical body is, however, quite small, while his heart, which regulates the life of that body, is in a mystical sense capable of comprehending the "Light in Extension" of the Sun of his being, which is the soul.

Thus Man is composed of body, soul, and spirit, and the soul is the mediator between the spiritual and material.

The Universe is composed of Malkuth and Kether, with Tiphereth as the Mediator between them, while, in a still greater sense we may consider Nuit and Hadit, the Two Infinites, with the Whole Living manifested Universe of Ra-Hoor-Khuit, as their Ever-Coming Son, the Crowned Child and Lord of the Aeon.

The Tree of Life is embedded in the Snowflake, its branches are as Crystals, it flowers as the Rose, and its perfect fruit is the Dodecahedron.
                              FRATER ACHAD.

CHAPTER I

IN THE NAME OF THE ONE, by the Grace of God Triune, and by the Favour and Appointing of the Ever-Coming Son, I will now endeavour to expound that which has been revealed unto me.

First, let me state my conviction that this Universe is the Perfect Work of a Perfect Being, and that any apparent imperfections are due to the limitations of our finite consciousness, so that even these contribute to the larger Perfection of the Whole.

Secondly, I believe there is a Supreme and Perfect Order in all things, in spite of any apparent disorder which, again, is but the result of restrictions in man himself.

Thirdly, that the essence of Order consists in the perfect adjustment of parts in subservience to the ends of the Whole, so that that which is most complex is most perfect, but that this very complexity is due to the combination of a few Ultimate Ideas which go to make up the One Thought of the Supreme Being.

I am inclined to believe that the perfection of the existing Universe is Progressive, insofar as the Whole may be said to expand and become more and more complex and greater and greater in extent while still in accord with the One Order which prevails from its most minute atom to its inconceivably vast circumference.

I incline to believe that the finite universe is not spherical, though tending ever to become so as its substance materializes. In other words that the Light precedes the Life which is its Substance, and the Life precedes the material which is *its* substance. Thus the rays of Light may spread out in the form of a Star, while the Ever-becoming Life and material substance tend to expand as a Sphere. The projecting rays, so to speak, drive back the primal chaos more easily than would a smooth sphere which expanded equally all over its surface. That such a conception implies at least a possibility, I shall presently endeavour to show.

There is another important point which should be mentioned. The Spiritual World of Ideas is in Perfect Order; the Material World of Substance is in Perfect Order; the Soul of the World, and of Man, which is the result of these, is capable of comprehending that Order perfectly.

But, again, the spirit of Man is perfect, his body is made in the Image and Likeness of God and of the Universe, but his soul, having within it the power of personal choice, or will, which alone enables him to progress in a free and intelligent manner, is at the same time liable to distortion if the personal will is ill-used or restricted. In that case the Eye of the soul sees things out of proportion and order, and this astigmatism must be corrected. Otherwise, man is under an illusion, self-created, which, however, in no way interferes with the Real Order of the Universe, but merely tends to confine him and to prevent him from enjoying his due heritage in all its fulness.

Thus the Great Work for Man consists in the adjustment of the soul, or Intellectual Sphere, so that it bears a perfect resemblance and correspondence to the Material and Natural Order of the Universe and at the same time exhibits its relation with the Supreme or Archetypal Order.

This possibility of distortion in the soul of man has led him into the direst troubles, but unless that soul were

THE BODY OF GOD

thus plastic it could not expand and take on the complex Design of the Greater Universe. Man's work consists in building up his soul by means of his personal will and creative imagination, under the guidance and direction of the Will of the Universe, into the same Archetypal Pattern which is to be found in the One Thought of God.

But how shall man discover this Design upon the Trestleboard of the Grand Architect? He may at least make an intelligent attempt to do so, as we shall endeavour to show.

Since perfect Order consists in a right relation, adjustment, and proportion of all the parts in subservience to the Idea of the Whole, we must first consider some of the necessary requirements of that Order.

The "Tree of Life" of the Qabalists has been called the "Minutum Mundum" or "Little Universe," and students of the Qabalah will have become aware that this system has great possibilities as a convenient means of classification in regard to every thing in the Universe, or idea in the mind of man. The Universe, for each one of us, consists of what we are able to comprehend of it. Some are content to feel themselves at-one with a very limited part; others realize that if once they could obtain the true Design, all would become possible of comprehension in a spiritual manner. But this Design has been lost, or so it seemed.

In Book 4, Part III—still in ms.—we may read: "An excellent man of great intelligence, a learned Qabalist, once amazed FRATER PERDURABO by stating that the Tree of Life was the framework of the Universe. It was as if some one had seriously maintained that a cat was a creature constructed by placing the letters C-A-T in that order. It is no wonder that Magick has excited the ridicule of the unintelligent, since even its educated students can be guilty of so gross a violation of the first principles of common sense."

I may state that I have not the slightest idea who this excellent man was, and that I have a good deal of respect for the opinions of Frater Perdurabo, but, at the risk of falling under the same stigma as this "unknown warrior" I shall break a lance with Frater Perdurabo on this point, before this treatise is completed.

Meanwhile, let me refer Students of the Holy Qabalah to the various designs of the Tree of Life which may be in their possession, or readily available.

Let us examine, for instance, those shown in Westcott's "Introduction to the Study of the Kabalah," Mather's translation of the "Kabbalah Unveiled," Pike's "Morals and Dogma," Inman's "Ancient Faiths," "The Equinox," Volume One, Number 2, page 243, Waite's "Doctrine and Literature of the Kabalah," Ginsburg's treatise on the subject, the Frontispiece to Book 777, the oldest extant design in the British Museum, etc., and we shall notice one very striking thing: They all vary greatly in their *proportions*. Some, it will be seen, are long and thin, others short and squatty. 777 alone gives a well proportioned Tree.

It would seem that this important aspect of proportion has received little or no attention in the past. But let me once again refer you to the ancient "Sepher Yetzirah" (as I did in regard to the arrangement of the Paths in "Q.B.L."); in it we are told to "Fix the Design in its Purity," to "Replace the Formative Power upon His Throne," or to "Restore the Device or Workmanship to its Place."

Was the author of that old treatise using mere idle words, or did he mean what he said? It is possible he did not know how to do this himself, since the mss. of the "Sepher Yetzirah" contain no diagrams of the "Tree of Life"; but, in

THE BODY OF GOD

any event, we may at least attempt to follow his lead and try, if possible, to discover more Light from a study of the *true proportions* of the Tree.

The formation of the "Tree of Life" is entirely geometrical, and as might be expected, we find the simplest elements of geometry as its basis: The Point, the Line, the Circle, the Triangle, and Right-angled figures.

The proper method of finding the correct centres of the Ten Sephiroth, and thus the points connected by the Paths, is as follows: Upon a vertical straight line of convenient length, describe with unchanged compasses four circles, the centre of each being on the line, the point where the upper arc of the lowest circle cuts the line forming the centre of the circle above, and so on.[1] Thus:

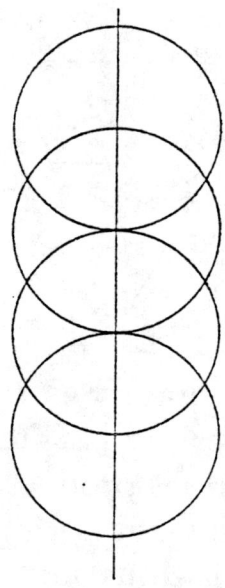

Figure I

---
[1] This method was pointed out to me some years ago by Frater Nubem Eripiam who claimed to have just discovered it. The method of construction as given in Liber 777, although producing a correctly proportioned Tree, does not show the generating circles, and is not nearly so simple in use.

The centre of the top circle gives the central Point of Kether, the intersections of the first and second circles form the centres of Chokmah and Binah, the centre of the third circle is Tiphereth, the intersections of the third and fourth circles indicate Netzach and Hod, the centre of the fourth circle is Yesod, and the lower point of its intersection with the vertical line is Malkuth.

This method produces a perfectly proportioned Figure of the Tree of Life, and the connecting Paths can all be made by joining the various points, thus:

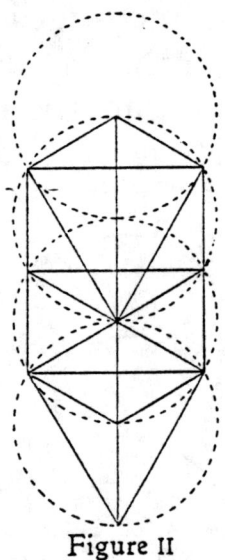

Figure II

In Freemasonry, Geometry is referred to as the "first and noblest of the Sciences" and as "the head of all learning." One of the simplest figures is produced by the intersection of two circles, thus forming what is known as the *Vesica Piscis*.

The curious and marvelous properties of the *Vesica Piscis* and of the Rectangle formed on its length and breadth, have been subjects of profound speculation, and perhaps nowhere have they been better described than in the "Magister-Mathesios" by our learned Brother Sydney T. Klein. I am sure

THE BODY OF GOD

he will have no objection if I quote a few passages from his work,[1] which has been one of the means of opening up before me such marvelous vistas.

After discussing the properties of the Masonic Square, obtained from the right-angled triangle by means of mundane measures of 3, 4, and 5 units to each side, respectively, he points out that a wave of wonderful enthusiasm must have swept across the civilized world when they first discovered that the Geometrical way of creating a right angle as given in Euclid I, 11, was by means of an Equilateral Triangle, by joining the vertex with the centre of the base. "This Equilateral Triangle" he writes, "was the earliest symbol, in connection with the Vesica Piscis, we know of the Divine Logos and, as the Bible declared that the Universe was created by the Logos (the Word) so the form of the Lodge which represents the Universe was naturally created by means of the Equilateral Triangle. A great mystery this must have appeared to those who, like the Hellenic philosophers, postulated that everything on earth has its counterpart in heaven, and who, in their religious mysticism, were always looking for signs of the transcendental in their temporal surroundings.

"But in what awe and reverence must they have held Geometry when they further found that the Equilateral Triangle was itself generated, as in the *first* problem of Euclid, upon which the whole Science of Geometry was therefore based, by the intersection of two circles.

"This figure was not only looked upon as a symbol of the Three Divine *personæ*, but that part of the figure which is bounded by the arcs of the two circles and which takes

---

[1] Trans. Quatuor Coronati Lodge, vol. xxiii, 1910, pp. 107-151.

to itself one-third of each of the two generating circles (making its perifera exactly equal with that remaining to each of the two circles, all three therefore being *co-equal*), and in which the triangle is formed, was naturally held from earliest times as the most sacred Christian emblem, namely that of *regeneration* or *new birth*. To show the extraordinary reverence and high value attached to this symbol, it is only necessary to remember that from the fourth century onwards all Seals of Colleges, Abbeys and other religious communities, as well as of ecclesiastical persons, have been made invariably of this form and they continue to be made so to this day. It was also in allusion to this most ancient emblem that Tertullian and the other early Fathers speak of Christians of 'Pisciculi.' It was called the 'Vesica

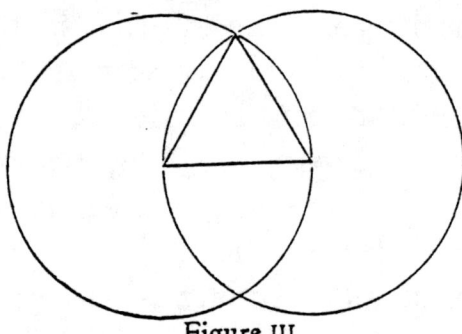

Figure III

Piscis' (Fish's bladder) and named such no doubt for the same reason as led the learned Rabbi Maimonides in the twelfth century, when dealing with a similar religious subject, to command his hearers: 'When you have discovered the meaning thereof, do not divulge it, because the people cannot philosophize or understand that to the infinite there is no such thing as sex.'

"The Vesica Piscis is intimately connected with the discovery by Augustus Caesar, as narrated by Baronius, of a prophecy in one of the Sybilline books foretelling 'a great

THE BODY OF GOD

event coming to pass in the birth of One who should prove to be the true "King of Kings," and that Augustus therefore dedicated an altar in his palace to the "unknown God."'"

Brother Klein then goes on to show how the Vesica Piscis was the true foundation of Gothic Architecture, and that its influence accounts for the sudden change from the old Norman style, which was based on the properties of the square rather than the triangle.

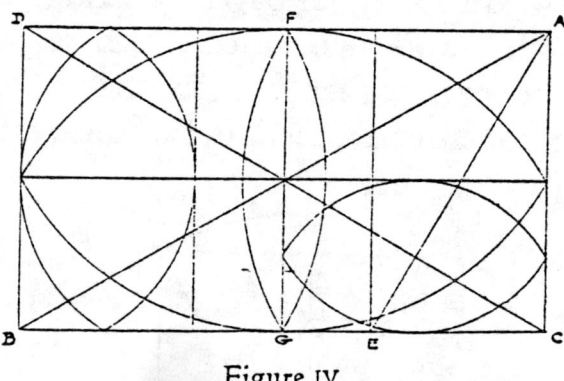

Figure IV

He then discloses some of the great wonders of the Vesica Piscis and points out: "The rectangle formed by the length and breadth of this mysterious figure in its simplest form has several extraordinary qualities; it may be cut into three equal parts, by straight lines parallel to its shorter sides:

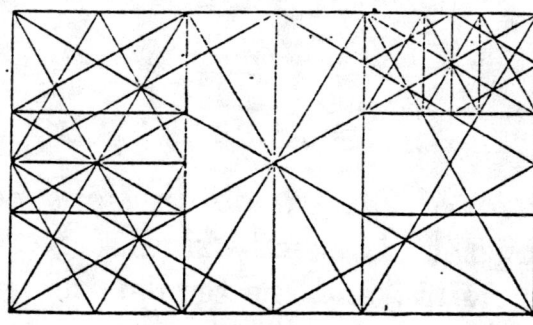

Figure V

and these parts will all be precisely and geometrically similar to each other and to the whole figure, strangely applicable to the Symbolism attached at that time to the Trinity in Unity, and this sub-division may be proceeded with indefinitely without making any change in form; however often the operation is performed the parts remain identical with the original figure, having all its extraordinary properties, and *no other rectangle* can have this curious property. It may also be cut into four equal parts by straight lines parallel to the two sides, and again each of these parts will be exactly similar to each other and to the whole, and the process may be continued indefinitely, the equilateral triangle appearing everywhere:

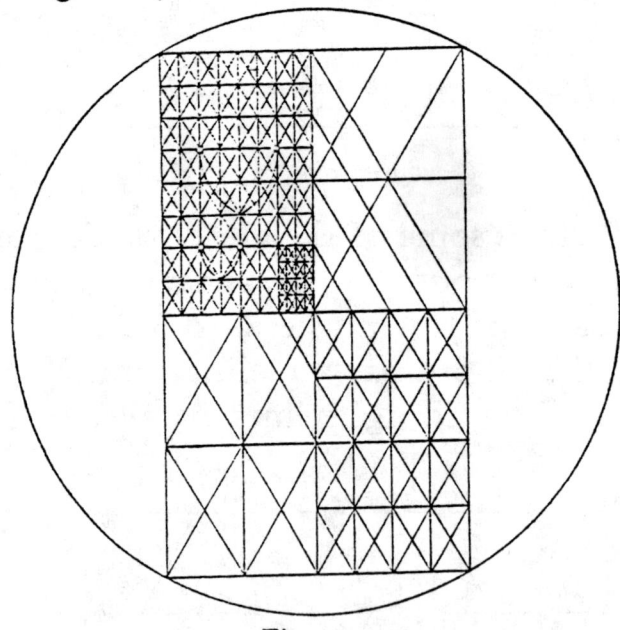

Figure VI

Once more, if two of the tri-sub-divisions be taken, the form of these together is exactly similar geometrically to half the original figure, and the equilateral triangle again appears everywhere in both; as in figure V.

THE BODY OF GOD

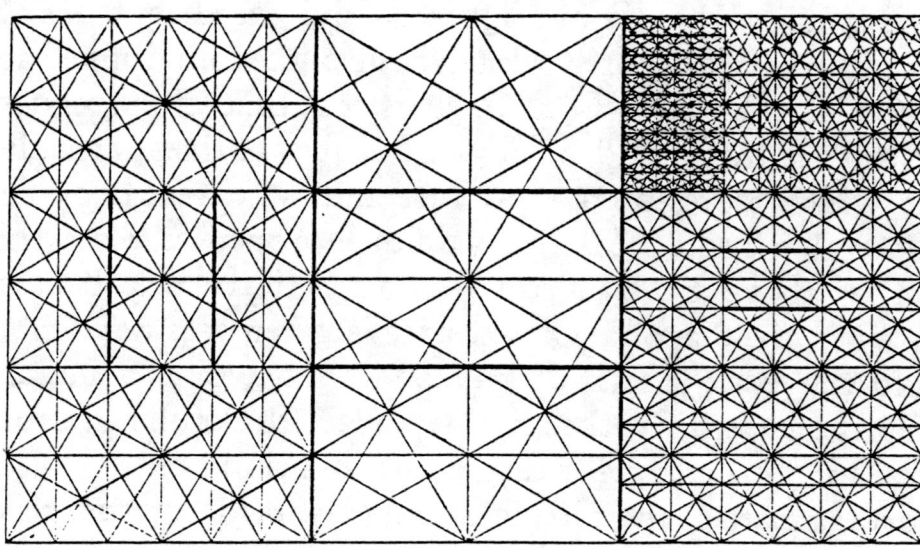

Figure VII

In Figure VII I have carried the tri-sub-division to the sixth degree, and to help the eye I have marked with darker lines one of the tri-sub-divisions of each degree; it is only owing to the above unique similarity that the equilateral triangle is again formed on every part of the base line. Again the diagonal is exactly double the length of its shorter side, which characteristic is also *unique* and greatly increases its use for plotting out designs, and this property, of course, holds good for all the rectangles formed by both species of sub-division, but perhaps its most mysterious property (though not of any practical use) to those who studied geometry, and to whom the figure was a Symbol of the Divine Trinity in Unity, was the fact that it actually put into their hands the means of trisecting the right angle. Now the three great problems of antiquity which engaged the attention of geometricians throughout the Middle Ages were *'the Duplication of a Cube,' 'the squaring of the Circle,'* and lastly, *'the trisection of an angle,'* even Euclid being unable to show how to do it, and yet it will be *seen* that the diagonal A B of Figure IV and the diagonal A E of the subsidiary figure, which is also the plumbline, actually trisect the angle D A C. It is true that it only shows how to trisect one kind of angle, but it was that particular angle which represented the Craft and was created by the equilateral triangle. All these unique properties place this figure far above that of a square for practical work, because even when the diagonal of a square is given it is impossible to find the exact length of any of its sides, or *vice versa.*"

I have quoted Brother Sydney Klein thus fully in order to give him due credit for his detailed working on this most important matter, and also to supply the reader with a clear idea of the unique features of these symbols, as well as of their deep religious significance and the actual effect that their practical application produced on all the religious Architecture of the Gothic period. On this basis many of the most important Cathedrals and Churches were erected, and their Beauty is not to be denied. When we compare some of these beautiful Gothic structures with the Pyramid, for instance, we cannot but notice the difference; but after all the Pyramid is a truly Symbolic structure in every detail, while the Gothic Cathedrals only show part of the truth.

Imagine my overwhelming joy when I discovered that the ancient Qabalistic Tree of Life, with all its wonderful possibilities as a means of mental classification of every idea in the Universe—Natural, Human and Divine—*was in its entirety based upon the same fundamental principle of the Vesica Piscis*, and was therefore *not a fixed design* but capable of indefinite *progression towards the Infinitely Small or the Infinitely Great.* For it can be so drawn that it appears with all its details and properties, repeating themselves indefinitely in every direction of Space to Infinity.

THE BODY OF GOD

Imagine what it means to a Qabalist who has arranged all the ideas in his mind, in duly Balanced and Equilibrated formation, to discover a way of perpetuating in thought all these Ideas, and to be able to realize that the "Tree of Life" upon which they are based is a LIVING TREE, with its Roots in the Infinitely Small and its Branches and Fruits extending to the furthest Limits of the Universe.

This is the nature of the discovery, or revelation, which came to me on April 14th, and it will form the subject of our further studies and researches.

CHAPTER II

EFORE discussing in detail the events which led up to this discovery, and the further application of it to the Tree of Life, it will be well if we spend a little time in considering the Nature of the Trinity, and its fundamental relation to all Systems of Religious and Philosophic thought.

Hermes the Thrice Greatest, like Solomon, is highly celebrated by antiquity for his wisdom and skill in the secret operations of nature, and for his *reputed discovery of the quintessential perfectibility of the three kingdoms in their homogeneal unity;* whence he is called the Thrice Great Hermes, having the *spiritual intelligence of all things in their universal law.*[1]

It is to be regretted that no one of the many books attributed to him, and which are named in detail by Clemens Alexandrinus, escaped the destroying hand of Diocletian.[2]

But we have one truly authentic record in the famous Emerald Tablet, which contains the one sole dogma of Hermetic Philosophy: "That which is above is as that which is below, and that which is below is as that which is above, for performing the miracles of the One Thing."

The Emerald Tablet, unique and authentic as it may be regarded, is all that remains to us from Egypt of her

---

[1] See Tertullianus de Anima, cap. ii. adversus Valentinianus, cap. xv. Hermetem vocat Physicorum Magistrum.
[2] Atwood. The Hermetic Mystery.

THE BODY OF GOD

Sacred Art. A few riddles and fables, all more or less imperfect, that were preserved by the Greeks, and some inscrutable hieroglyphics, are still to be found quoted in certain of the alchemical records; but the originals are entirely lost.

There is little doubt that Ancient Egypt did at one time hold the true Key of the Mysteries. For what did Pythagoras, Thales, Democritus and Plato become immured there for several solitary years, but to be initiated in the wisdom and learning of those Egyptians? Yet Hermes himself is reported to have prophesied her fall, and the loss of her wisdom and learning; and this certainly was fulfilled. But, as I have endeavoured to point out in my treatise, "The Egyptian Revival," there seems every reason to suppose that in this New Aeon, during this Aquarian Age, man will once more come into his own, and be directly informed by the true Spirit of Wisdom and Understanding in a way that has not been possible for many Ages. At least there seems every hope of the revival of the Universal Tradition of the Golden Age, despite the present world-crisis and the breaking up of the old civilization. But it is necessary that things should be destroyed in order that they may be renewed, as the Justified Osiris said in regard to His Body. So it is, perhaps, in regard to our pre-conceived ideas of the Body of the Universe, or of the Tree of Life, or some other pet theory; but so long as we receive something better in exchange for that with which we must part, what matter!

There is certainly no denying the importance of the "Three in One," as far as Hermes is concerned, for his very title of Thrice Greatest implies in what veneration such conceptions must have been held in his day.

In Alchemy we find three Principles—Sulphur, Mercury, and Salt; and Three great Stages of the Work—the

Discovery of the Formation of the Stone of the Wise, its Multiplication, and its Projection. These later stages have been very little understood.

In the Qabalah (from the three-lettered root QBL, meaning "To Receive") we find mention of the Sacred Three Lettered Name of God IHV, implying the Father, Mother, and Son. We find Three Mother Letters in the Hebrew Alphabet, Aleph, Mem and Shin, and these are in turn attributed to the Three Elements, Air, Water and Fire, which correspond to the Alchemical Principles, and in admixture form Earth, or The Stone. We also find in the Sepher Yetzirah, the oldest Qabalistic treatise, that the "One created the Universe by means of the Three Sepharim, Number, Writing and Speech." These correspond to the Three Mother Letters and to the Three Paths of the Middle Pillar of the Tree, as I have shown in "Q.B.L."

The Hindus venerate the Three-letterd Word AUM as the most sacred Name of God; their Deity has Three Aspects as Brahma, Vishnu, and Shiva; the Creator, Preserver, and Destroyer. They postulate Three Principles, Rajas, Tamas, and Sattva, or Activity, Inertia, and Peace.

The Christians believe in Three Persons in One God; The Father, Son, and Holy Spirit; in Three that bear witness in Heaven, and in Three that bear witness on Earth. That man is three-fold; Body, Soul, and Spirit.

In fact the Importance of the Number Three, and of the Triangle, is a well nigh inexhaustible subject.

Many of these three-fold Ideas are summed up in a Fourth, representing the Materialized or Manifested aspect.

The Sides of the Pyramid are Triangular, but its Base is Square. The Word AUM is made continuous in sound by the addition of the nasal N, forming AUMN. The He-

THE BODY OF GOD

brew IHV, becomes IHVH through the addition of the final Hé, or the Daughter. The Archetypal, Creative, and Formative Worlds become Manifest in Assiah, the Material World of the Qabalah. The tripartite Word INR, becomes INRI. The Trinity of Triads of the Tree of Life are summed up in the Single Sphere of Malkuth, the Kingdom. Sulphur, Mercury, and Salt produce the Gold of the Alchemist. Rajas, Tamas, and Sattva act on Prakriti.

Three and Four together make Seven, another sacred Number, as everyone knows.

Seven and three are Ten, and this is said to be the most Sacred and Complete of all, since it represents a return from One to the Primal Nothing of the Beginning. We find Ten Sephiroth on the Qabalistic Tree. The Four letters of the Sacred Name IHVH, when arranged in the form of a Triangle, make 10, thus:

Figure VIII

and this became the basis of the Tetractys of Pythagoras, a figure composed of Ten Unit forms or Yods.

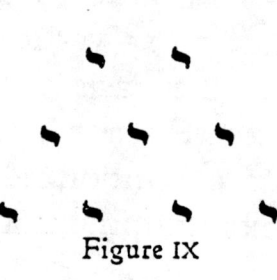

Figure IX

But here we begin to approach the Central Mystery once more, for this Triangle, with its ten Dots, gives us the idea of the Division of the triangle into others, thus:

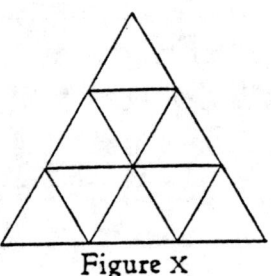

Figure X

and so we begin to get back to our Equilateral Triangle and Vesica as the Basis of the Tree of Life. But there is another interesting fact, viz.:—that an Equilateral Triangle, so divided, having a base of, say, three inches, will contain nine triangles, the sides of which will each be one inch. Whereas a Square, whose side is three inches, will also contain exactly the same number of one inch squares, viz.: nine.

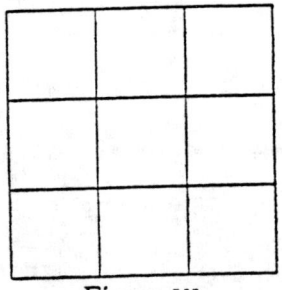

Figure XI

Again the numbers 1-9 may be so arranged in the nine squares, that they will add to 15 vertically, horizontally and diagonally. This forms the basis for the construction of the Magick Squares of the Planets, etc.

But all these ideas are symbolized in the Tree of Life itself, which we will next examine in further detail.

THE BODY OF GOD

CHAPTER III

THE "Sepher Yetzirah," or Book of Formation, which is perhaps the oldest philosophical treatise as yet extant in the Hebrew language, opens as follows:

"In two and thirty most occult and wonderful paths of wisdom, did IAH, the Lord of Hosts, engrave his name . . . He created this universe by the three Sepharim, Number, Writing, and Speech.

"Ten are the numbers, as are the Sephiroth, and twenty-two the letters; these are the Foundation of all things. Of these letters, three are mothers, seven are double, and twelve are simple.

"The ten numbers formed from nothing, are the Decad; these are seen in the fingers of the hands, five on one, five on the other, and over them is the Covenant by voice spiritual, and the rite of Circumcision, corporeal (as of Abraham).

"Ten are the numbers of the ineffable Sephiroth, *ten and not nine, ten and not eleven.* Learn this wisdom, and be wise in the understanding of it; investigate these numbers, and draw *knowledge* from them; fix the design in its purity, and pass from it to its Creator seated on his throne." (Dr. Westcott's translation.)

It is well to notice that the ancient Qabalists made a particular point of the fact that there are TEN Sephiroth, neither more nor less. If we examine the formation of the "Tree of Life" in the following Figure (XII), we shall understand why they were so careful to make this plain.

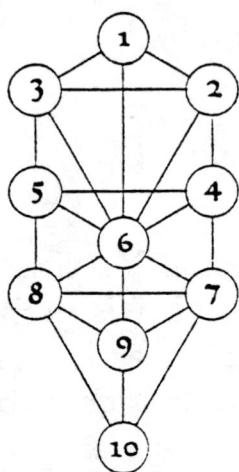

Figure XII

One might at first be inclined to suppose that there should be another Sephira in the centre of the upper hexagon, and this is, as a matter of fact, the location assigned to the Sphere of DAATH, or Knowledge, as the child of Chokmah and Binah. But it is not to be shown on the plan of the Tree for it represents a Higher Dimensional Knowledge, which should be drawn from the whole Tree, as it is written, "Draw knowledge from them." Should such a Sphere be shown in the design, it would also necessitate extra "Paths" leading thereto, but we are clearly told that the Paths of Wisdom are thirty-two in all, that is to say, the Ten Numerical Emanations and their connecting links formed by the Twenty-two letters.

Likewise we notice that there are no paths from 2 to 5 and from 3 to 4 or from 1 to 4 and 1 to 5. Had there been, we should see the symbol of the upright Pentagram, which is the Star of unconquered Will in the Microcosm, united with the Sign of the Hexagram of the Macrocosm. But this unification represents the Great Work which must be accomplished by man, and it is part of the Universal Plan

THE BODY OF GOD

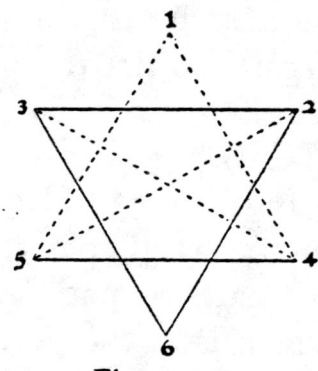

Figure XIII

that he should discover their equivalence for himself in order that he may become a conscious co-operator in the Divine Scheme of Creation. Therefore we find an "Abyss," and no direct connecting link between Binah and Chesed.

Again, one might be tempted to suppose that there should be three averse equilateral triangles, 2-6-3, 4-9-5, and 7-10-8. But should 4-9 and 5-9 be connected by paths, a figure of the evil and averse Pentagram with its two points uppermost, would appear upon the tree; thus:

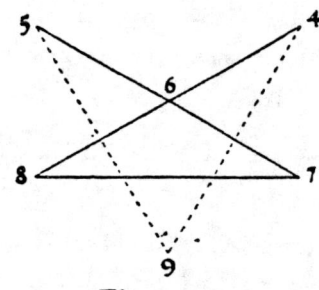

Figure XIV

We must do nothing, then, which will in any way interfere with the arrangement as it stands, for it is a veritable Work of Wisdom.

Let us again examine the arrangement and juxtaposition of the Paths as shown in figure XII. It will be noticed that the Hexagon bounded by 1-2-4-6-5-3, is perfect in form; all its sides are equal. That the Triangles 2-3-6 and 7-8-10 are perfectly equilateral. That the triangles 1-2-3, 2-4-6, 3-5-6, 4-5-6, 7-6-8, 7-9-8, 7-9-10, and 8-9-10, are all equal and have an angle of 120 Degrees or exactly one-third of a circle. That the small triangles 4-6-7 and 5-6-8 are both equilateral. That the paths connecting 6-7-9-8 produce a diamond which is in the proportion of a perfect Vesica.

It should further be noticed that the two rectangles, 3-2-4-5 and 5-4-7-8 are each exactly based on the proportion of the Vesica, so that they partake of all the properties shown in figure V, as explained in detail by Brother Klein.

If the breadth of the Tree be taken as the Length of One Vesica, the height from the centre of Malkuth to the centre of Kether is exactly the Width of Four such Vesicæ.

The Path from Kether to Tiphereth is exactly equal to the combined lengths of the two paths of the Middle Pillar between Tiphereth and Malkuth. Further study on the part of the Student will disclose many other proportions.

The learned but anonymous author of "The Canon," published by Elkin Mathews in 1897, makes several important statements in regard to the Vesica Piscis and its relation to the Mysteries of the Qabalah, Architecture, etc. He writes: "It is known, both to freemasons and architects, that the mystical figure called the Vesica Piscis, so popular in the Middle Ages, and generally placed as the first proposition of Euclid, was a symbol applied by the masons in planning their temples. Albert Dürer, Serlio, and other architectural writers depict the Vesica in their works, but presumably because of an unspeakable mystery attached to it, these authors make no reference to it. Thomas Kerrich, a freemason and principal librarian of the University of Cambridge, read a paper upon this mystical figure before the Society of Antiquaries on January 20, 1820. He illustrated his remarks with many diagrams illustrating its use by the ancient masons, and piously concludes by saying: 'I would by no means indulge in conjectures as to the reference these figures might possibly have to the most sacred mysteries of religion.' Dr. Oliver ("Discrep." p. 109), speaking of the Vesica, says: 'This mysterious figure Vesica Piscis possessed an unbounded influence on the details of sacred architecture; and *it constituted the great and enduring secret of our ancient brethren.* The plans of religious buildings were determined by its use; and the proportions of length and height were dependent on it alone.' Mr. Clarkson (Introductory Essay to Billings' "Temple Church") considered that the elementary letters of the primitive language were derived from the same mystical symbol. He says that it was known to Plato and 'his masters in the Egyptian colleges' and was to the old builders 'an archetype of ideal beauty.' The Vesica was also regarded as a baneful object under the name of 'Evil Eye,' and the charm most generally employed to avert the dread effects of its fascination was the Phallus (J. Millinger's "Archaelogia," XIX). In Heraldry, the Vesica was used as the feminine shield. It was interchangeable with the Fusill, or Mascle, and was also figured as a lozenge or rhombus. In the East the Vesica was used as a symbol of the womb, and was joined to the cross by the Egyptians forming the handle of the Crux Ansata.

"Geometrically, the Vesica is constructed from two intersecting circles, so that it may be taken as having a double significance. Edward Clarkson says that it 'means astronomically at the present day a starry conjunction; and by a very intelligent transfer of typical ideas a divine marriage,' or the two-fold essence of life, which the ancients supposed to be male and female. To every Christian the Vesica is familiar from its constant use in early art, for not only was it an attribute of the Virgin, and the feminine aspect of the Saviour as symbolized by the *wound* in his side, but it commonly surrounds the figure of Christ, as His Throne when seated in Glory. As a hieroglyphic the combination of Christ with the Vesica is analogous to the Crux Ansata of the Egyptians."

A little further on in his book the author of "The Canon" also makes the following remarks: "Geometrically, the diagram containing the ten steps of the Cabala is shown by Kircher and other authorities in the form ascribed by Freemasons to what they call the 'Double Cube,' that is to

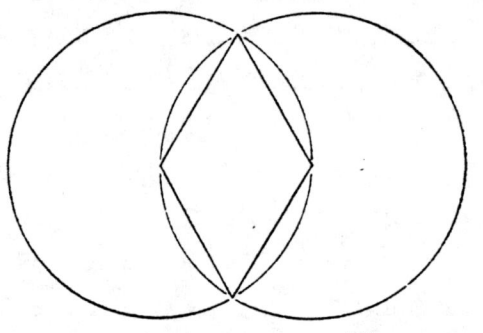 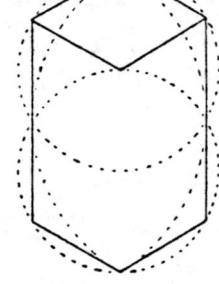

Figure XV

say, an irregular hexagon, which will exactly enclose a Vesica. *Consequently its length and breadth are of the proportion of 26 to 15.* It is said that the ten cabalistic steps, in their entirety, symbolize the aspect of the Deity expressed by the four mystic letters IHVH, whose numerical value is 26. This number was said by the Jews to comprise the most sacred mysteries of the Law. No explanation, how-

THE BODY OF GOD

ever, has ever been given showing how the number 26 afforded a key to all the science of the Israelites. *It is now suggested that the Vesica, whose proportion is in the ratio of 26 to 15, was the symbol of the hidden rule or canon, by which the synthesis of nature was reduced to a comprehensible figure, capable of demonstrating to initiates the truth and knowledge which constituted the sacred wisdom of antiquity."*

The last sentence is of much interest in the light of our present researches. I had not noticed this reference when first writing this book, but it is not alone a confirmation of our general ideas, but leads to others of importance.

Brother Klein gives the true proportion of the Vesica Piscis as that of 8 to 13.85, but probably the nearest in whole numbers is that above given by the author of The Canon, viz.: 15 to 26. (I think the exact proportion is 15.01 to 26.)[1] Now these numbers 26 and 15 are of great Qabalistic value. 26, as stated by the author of the "Canon," is the numeration of IHVH, and this, as shown in "Q.B.L." and elsewhere, is the "Formula" upon which the whole System is based. 15 is the numeration of IH or "Jah," the venerable Name of God, attributed in the "Sepher Yetzirah" to the Creator Who devised the Thirty-two Paths of Wisdom which we are discussing.

---

[1] The neatest formula indicating the exact proportions of the Vesica is as One is to the Square Root of Three ($1:\sqrt{3}$). This also is very symbolic for it shows the Unity in its relation to a certain aspect of the Trinity, while since the numbers represented are 1 and 3, it is strongly suggestive of 13 = AChD = Unity.

The above is actually more accurate mathematically than 15:26, for $1:\sqrt{3}::1:1.732$, while $15:26::1:1.733$. But there is always likely to be some slight difference between mathematical accuracy and a general Magical formula, as witness the word ALHIM (Elohim) which suggests Pi as 3.1415 whereas 3.1416 is more correct. I hardly know of a Magical formula in fractions unless it be 6/50 = 0.12, for which see Liber Legis and Comment.

The author of the "Canon" makes a valuable suggestion when he remarks that the *length* and *breadth* of the Tree of Life are as 26 to 15, although his statement is not actually correct. Qabalistically, however, we may notice a very interesting thing. The Total numeration of Sephiroth of the Middle Pillar, or length of the Tree, is $1 + 6 + 9 + 10 = 26$, while the two Sephiroth forming the bases of the side pillars, and indicating the breadth of the Tree are, Netzach $= 7$ and Hod $= 8$, thus $7 + 8 = 15$.

Now although the Vesica Piscis is the hidden rule or canon upon which the figure is built, the true proportion of the Tree is much more wonderful than if its length and breadth were in the proportion of a simple Vesica. As explained before, the true proportion is that of the width of four Vesicæ in *height* to the length of one Vesica in *width*. This suggests the "Four Worlds" of the Qabalah. But since the rectangle bounding a Vesica may be divided into three equal parts by lines parallel to the shorter sides, and the divisions thus formed are found each to have the same proportions as the original figure, we shall also find that *three* out of the four parts of the height of the Tree of Life will represent the exact length of a Vesica the breadth of which is equal to the breadth of the Tree from centre to centre of the Sephiroth forming the side pillars. To make this plainer: if we take the reciprocal path from Chesed to Geburah as equivalent to 26 (it being the length of one of the four vesicæ and at the same time the width of the Tree) and construct thereon another Vesica we shall find that its highest and lowest points will be in the centres of Kether and Yesod. Thus the first Nine Sephiroth are in exact proportion of the Vesica and Malkuth remains as a pendant. The height of this Vesica will now be 45 and its width 26. We have exam-

THE BODY OF GOD

ined the number 26 as to its mystical value, but 45 is found to be the mystic number of Yesod, which represents the generative organs. In addition to this we find that the sum of the numbers of the Sephiroth 1-9 is 45, and this is the numeration of ADM the Hebrew ADAM. Further if we notice the Vesica thus formed, it will be found to have its apex in Kether while the left hand curve cuts through the centre of Geburah and the right hand curve through that of Chesed, both these terminating in Yesod. Therefore these lines unite $1 + 4 + 5 + 9 = 19$. Now 19 is the numeration of ChVH, or Chavvah, which is the Hebrew word for EVE. Thus we find ADAM and EVE united; with IHVH in the midst of their union.

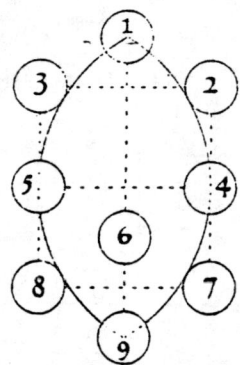

Figure XVI

The fact that we find these first Nine Sephiroth forming a perfect Vesica and producing such symbolism is indeed significant, and this coupled with the fact that we find the circle of Malkuth below this Vesica, and that Malkuth has been referred to the World of Shells or Excrement (Gross matter) and has been called The Un-Redeemed Daughter, is indeed a startling piece of natural symbolism.

But so far we have a Vesica and a Sphere pendant, and our Tree of Life is not fully represented in terms of Vesicæ.

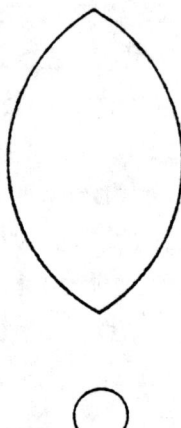

Figure XVII

The real mystery lies in the fact that just as in the first proposition of Euclid, the Vesica is formed by the *intersection of two circles,* so the true proportion of this figure is found to be that of the *intersection of two Vesicæ.* In which case the

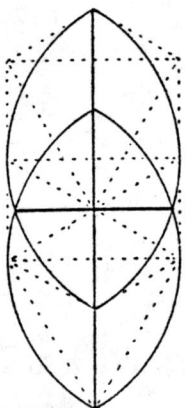

Figure XVIII

Upright line of the Middle Pillar represents the Father, the Horizontal line which runs through Tiphereth represents the Son, the Upper Vesica the Mother, and the lower one the Daughter. Thus we have the complete representation of IHVH in graphic form, and the exact proportions of the Tree of Life are shown.

THE BODY OF GOD

The foregoing properties, alone, make this Figure of the Tree of Life quite unique, but when we add its regular Qabalistic Correspondences as a symbolic universal basis of all Ideas, and a proper means of their classification in perfect Order, we are almost overwhelmed at the sublimity of the conception. But we have hardly begun to consider its possibilities in other directions. We have not as yet discussed the proper proportion of the Sephirotic Circles to the length of the Paths, but this matter will be taken up in detail later on. Meanwhile let us notice that the connecting Paths are *Lines* and the Sephiroth *Circles* (or Spheres). The Line and the Circle make up the Number 10, and also represent the Letters IO equivalent to the root of the God-name of Jove, who is identical with the Hebrew Jehovah.

Let us consider some of the statements of the Sepher Yetzirah in greater detail.

Firstly we find the words *"In two and thirty most occult and wonderful paths of wisdom, did IAH, the Lord of Hosts, engrave his name."* Let us consider the words *two* and *thirty*. Two is the numeration of the letter Beth, which is attributed to Mercury or Wisdom, and to the Magician or Occultist who controls the elemental forces. Thirty is "Lamed" or "Ox-Goad" or sharp pointed "engraver." It is also the letter of Libra or of Justice and Balance, so here in one letter we get the idea of the Scales with the tongue of the balance (or ox-goad) between them. The letters BL in Hebrew form the word meaning "Lord," while LB means "Mind" or "Heart." The Mind is the receptacle of Wisdom, and the Heart of Love and Will. The Number 32 is the numeration of AHIH the Divine Name of Kether, and IHVH the Ineffable Name ruling the other Nine Sephiroth, coalesced, in the Great Name AHIHVH which embraces the whole Ten in One. The Name IAH is in Hebrew Yod-hé, or IH and this is called the Monogram of the Eternal. The letters are the first two of IHVH and represent the Father and Mother conjoined and concealing the Son (A, the Microcosm or Star of Unconquered Will) within them. Yod is the letter of Fire, Hé of Water, and the concealed Aleph is Air. These are the natures of the three Sepharim, Number, Writing and Speech, by which Jah is said to have created the Universe. Number is Fire (the writing of the Stars), Writing flows like Water, and Air is the basis of Speech.

But these are all mysteriously connected symbolically with the Perfect Number 10, of which 0 is the Naught of the Unmanifest, and 1 the First Positive Idea. The Mouth from which issues the Fire of the Spirit in the form of Breath, and also the Water, is, when closed, a horizontal line. When open it is a Circle; thus, 10.

The Pen whereby Ideas are transmitted in the form of Writing, has been referred to in the Scriptures as "The Pen of a Man" and this is dipped in a vessel which represents both a line and a circle, for purposes of reproduction and transmission of form and substance. Thus we have the idea "IH" once more. Speech cometh from the Opening and Closing of the Mouth, thus by the combined ideas of 1 and 0 or 10. In the Tarot the Letter Aleph (1) is that of Air, and also of The Fool, which is marked Zero, or 0. Aleph is the Ox; Lamed, as mentioned above, is the Ox-goad, together they are AL, the most sacred Name of the One God, and LA which means "Not" or Zero which is 0. AL is numerically 31, suggesting the Three Sepharim in One and $3 + 1 = 4$; and the sum of the Numbers from $1 - 4 = 10$.

"Ten are the numbers, as are the Sephiroth, and twenty-two the letters, these are the Foundation of all things."

THE BODY OF GOD

Twenty is the numeration of the basic simple Hebrew Letter or IOD, spelt in full. Beth (2) is the House or Womb. Yod is equivalent to the spermatazoon in one sense. Twenty is also the numeration of the Hebrew Letter Kaph which means the palm of the hand in the act of grasping. Yod also means the Hand. So we have the chief instrument of action, the hand, in the act of opening and closing, representing expansion and contraction. 22 is the numeration of the word IChD which means Unity.

"Of these letters, three are mothers, seven are double, and twelve are simple." We have mentioned the three Mother Letters under the form of the Three Sepharim. These represent the Three Elements, which combined, form Earth. The Seven Double letters are assigned to the Seven Planetary Intelligences, the Forces which govern Nature; and the Twelve Simple letters are attributed to the Signs of the Zodiac, or Circle of Life, which represents the great Star Universe. Thus in the twenty-two letters we have the basis of all Universal Ideas. The One Substance with its three Elementary divisions combining in material form; the Planets and Solar System, the Star Universe, all permeated with the One Life which is the Subtle Substance of Light Itself.

The Three Mother Letters are equivalent to the Three Primary Colours, which break up into the Seven Colours of the Rainbow, and may be further divided into Twelve. So the Paths of the Tree represent all the Colours between Light and Darkness, and, of course, a host of other ideas as may be found in "Q.B.L." and Book 777.

The Book of Hermes, or Thoth, called the Tarot, contains Twenty-two symbolic Designs, which have been attributed to these Paths, and thus we may read in them the ancient Tradition by means of this Universal Alphabet of Symbols, as shown in my treatise "The Egyptian Revival."

"The ten numbers formed from nothing, are the Decad; these are seen in the fingers of the hands, five on one, five on the other, and over them is the Covenant by voice spiritual, and the rite of Circumcision, corporeal (as of Abraham)."

The Ten Sephiroth were said to have come from the AIN or Nothing; we have made some explanation of this in the Introduction. Reference is again made to the "hands" (which connect the idea of the Paths with that of the Sephiroth, as shown above). The hands represent the pairs of opposites, or balanced ideas, but these must always be united to find the point of equilibrium. They also represent two Pentagrams, or the Divine and Human Wills. When united in the strong grip of the Lion, these two five-fold stars meet in fellowship and harmony, as 10.

The peculiar statements about the Covenant by voice spiritual, and the rite of Circumcision, corporeal, are worthy of study. The Ideas are those of the great opposites, Spirit and Matter, which are ever united in the Sun of the Soul. But again the "voice" requires the opening of the "mouth" thus changing the horizontal line into a circle. The rite of circumcision has the effect of cutting away the "circle" of the foreskin, and disclosing the "vertical line" upon the head of the male organ. The organ itself represents a line, either vertical or horizontal, and this "rite" was for the purpose of making this organ safe from possible impurity, when connected with the "Circle." This act again is symbolic of the descent (or ascent) of Spirit into Matter, or the Harmonious union of Fire and Water, producing Air, which is in turn representative of the "Soul" or Mediator.

THE BODY OF GOD

With all this truly wonderful symbolism attached to the number 10, it is hardly surprising, if for no other reason, that the next verse of the Sepher Yetzirah makes it so clear that the Sephiroth are Ten, and not nine or eleven.

But this verse also tells us that after investigating these numbers, we must *"fix the design in its purity,"* so it is time we returned to our discussion of that subject.

CHAPTER IV

WE SHOULD remember that just as the Soul is the link between Body and Spirit, so is the Sun between Earth and Heaven, and the Great Central Sun between the Two Infinites. This Link between the Opposites is an all-important one, but it may be equally a Devil or Redeemer, according to the Influence it has upon us. I have showed this more fully elsewhere, and shall refer to it again.

Now we found the "Paths" symbolized a set of Universal Ideas, including all Colours. Likewise we shall find that the Ten Sephiroth have a corresponding Symbolism.

Malkuth, the 10th Sephira, is the Sphere of the Elements (corresponding to the Mother Letters); the next Seven above Malkuth are attributed to the Solar System (or Planets, the Double Letters); Chokmah, the next higher, is the Sphere of the Zodiac or Fixed Stars; and Kether is the Pure Light and the Source of All as the Primum Mobile or First Motion. So we see that in a certain sense the Ten Sephiroth are equal to the Twenty-two Paths, and in order to Fix the Design in its Purity, we must be able to arrange these Diverse Sets of Ideas so that they blend together perfectly. That at first may seem like an impossibility; in fact for several hundred years the Qabalists have adopted an arrangement which entirely failed to produce this perfect Harmony and Order.

THE BODY OF GOD

How I was led to discover such an arrangement, has been fully shown in "Q.B.L." written last year, and its further proof is given in "The Egyptian Revival" to which I may refer those interested.

The following figure is the completed result of those investigations:

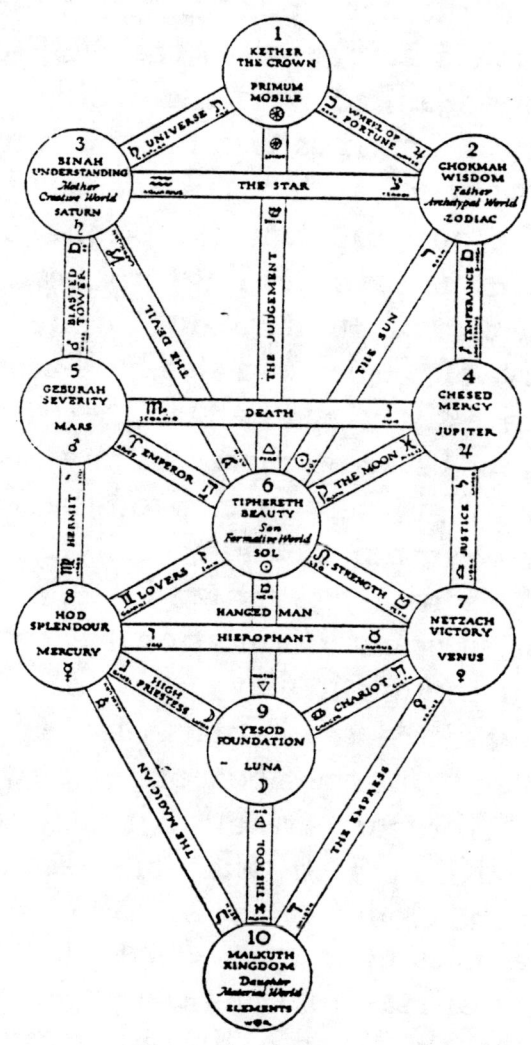

Figure XIX

It will be seen that the Paths of the Middle Pillar are made by the Three Mother Letters, which by shape form the Caduceus of Mercury, and these descending from Kether through the Sun and Moon (Tiphereth and Yesod) produce the Sphere of the Elements, or Malkuth. All the Planetary Letters except Kaph, which is attributed to Jupiter, the Father of the Gods, Io, will be seen to connect their Paths with the corresponding Planetary Sephiroth. The Twelve Letters attributed to the Signs of the Zodiac will each be found united with the Sephira of its Ruling Planet, even in cases such as Gemini and Virgo which are both ruled by Mercury; Libra and Taurus both ruled by Venus; etc. The one apparent exception (on account of the fact that all four paths leading to Chesed are properly occupied) is the case of Jupiter. But Jupiter, being the direct representative of Kether, and also by Tarot "The Wheel of Life," which exactly symbolizes the Primum Mobile, could not possibly be better placed in any case.

The fact that this Reformation of the Paths produces a wealth of fresh Symbolism and actually discloses the long lost Universal Tradition (as shown in "The Egyptian Revival") is alone sufficient justification for changing the arrangement, even though it may upset the ideas of certain people who have based the Rituals of their Secret Orders upon the old plan. But the Book of the Law, Liber Legis, clearly states: "Abrogate are all Rituals, all words and Signs; Ra-Hoor-Khuit hath taken His seat in the East at the Equinox of the Gods." (1904 E.V.)

But this becomes even more essential when we recognize the necessity of Harmonizing the Paths with the Sephiroth as explained above, and "Success is thy proof," since this change has led to such marvelous fresh developments

THE BODY OF GOD

as will be seen before this book is concluded. We may remark, to Qabalists, that this represents the true reconciliation of the "Snake" and the "Sword," thus removing both the "tempter" and the "avenger" from the Gate of Eden; to which we should now be able to return in safety, to our great joy and comfort.

To return once more to the "discovery" of April 14th, and the events which led up to it. I had been considering the Sun and all that It means to Humanity; how it is indeed the Golden Key to the Soul of the World, for this One Symbol contains in itself all "Trinities" of Symbolism. To the Soul of Mankind it has meant in the past all that is "good," all that is "evil," and all that is Divine and above these, according to the view taken by Man himself. The Sun is the True Son but the False Father. He is the Father of this Planet, but the Son of the Star Universe by Its Invisible Father. Those who worship the Sun (or Son) but fail to pass ON to the concealed Father, fall into "Sin" which is Restriction. Those who obtain "Solar Dhyana" and go no further, become fanatics, however wonderful their illumination may seem. Thus the Sun is at once an Angel of Light, the Devil, and the Redeemer. For the Son spake truly when He said "No man cometh unto the Father but by me," but the worship and Deification of the Son in place of the Father has proved fatal enough to those who misunderstood.

With these, and many similar thoughts in mind, I was contemplating the "Tree of Life" when I thought of the idea of temporarily removing the supports and reciprocal paths, and leaving the Sun connected with the Sephiroth by means of direct rays, thus:

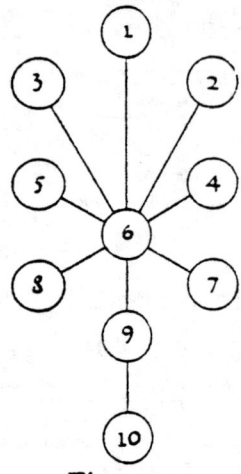

Figure XX

I then noticed a very interesting fact; that if, as it were, on the pivot of the Sun, the other Sephiroth were revolved and united, the result would be as follows: Kether would swing round and exactly cover Malkuth. Chokmah and Binah (Wisdom and Understanding) would unite and swing down so that their Circumference exactly half covered Malkuth and Kether, forming a Vesica as in the first Problem of Euclid. Chesed, Geburah, Netzach and Hod would all swing down and cover Yesod, so that the whole figure would fold up thus:

Figure XXI

This suggested to my mind, the idea of One Cell; first in process of Division, and then Divided except for a ray of Influence between the two. In other Words the Supreme

THE BODY OF GOD

Light one with Matter, dividing through Wisdom and Understanding, and becoming the Moon (Yesod) and Sun (Tiphereth). Or, The Sun and Moon uniting and producing the other symbolic ideas—who can say?

Then, seeing the Vesica thus formed, I was led to consider its relation to the "Tree" in general, and seeing all folded up between Tiphereth and Malkuth, I especially noticed the Paths from Netzach to Yesod, and from Hod to Yesod, and saw that if these were produced so that they crossed each other as far as the lower part of the Circumference of Yesod, they would become the GENERATING PATHS of another small "Tree" which would exactly extend from the Centre of Yesod (as its Kether) to the lowest point of the Circumference of Malkuth (as its Malkuth), thus bringing the Yesod of the "Little Tree" exactly in the Centre of Malkuth in the Larger one, and Tiphereth of the Small one exactly on the upper line of the circumference of the larger Malkuth.

It must be remarked that Yesod is said to be the representative of the Generative Organs, when the "Tree" is considered in regard to its correspondence to man, and that Netzach and Hod represent the twin Spheres connected therewith. Thus the discovery that these produced a "New Tree" was startling enough, till I began to realize that this process would go on indefinitely, the "Trees" giving birth to smaller and smaller ones toward the Infinitely Small or, conversely, expanding into greater and greater ones without Limit towards the Infinitely Great. Thus the Tree was the veritable Representative of Ra-Hoor-Khuit, Lord of the Aeon, the Ever Coming Son of the Two Infinites.

Therewith I gave Praise unto Ra-Hoor-Khuit, and became Silent as Harpocrates, the twin of Horus which is hidden within Him.

And I did well to be silent, for there was much more to be discovered (though I could not conceive it at the time). So I put aside the sketch of my first rough working, having signed and dated it, and left the matter alone for a while.

Herewith I include a drawing made from this first sketch, as a record of the discovery.

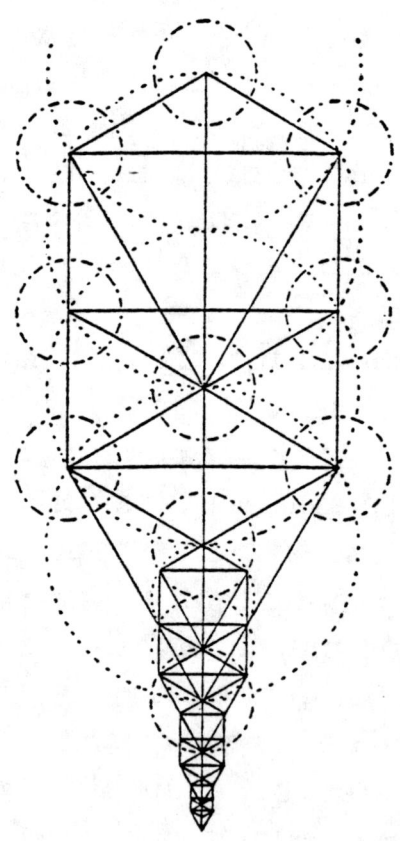

Figure XXII

THE BODY OF GOD

CHAPTER V

E MAY now begin to understand what was meant by the next few words of the "Sepher Yetzirah" which states: *"These Ten Numbers, beyond the universal One, have the boundless realms, boundless origin and end. . . ."*

But we may turn aside for a moment, at this point, and consider the old system of the Qabalah, as perpetuated and expounded by the best commentators of the past.

Mention is made of the "Four Worlds" of the Qabalah. These are called Atziluth, the Archetypal World; Briah, the Creative World; Yetzirah, the Formative World; and Assiah, the Material World. These have been attributed to the Four Letters of the Ineffable Name IHVH. Sometimes these worlds have been allotted to the "Tree of Life" as follows: Atziluth and Yod (the Father) to Chokmah; Briah and Hé (the Mother) to Binah; Yetzirah and Vau (the Son) to Tiphereth as the King ruling over Chesed, Geburah, Netzach, Hod and Yesod (thus embracing six Sephiroth); and finally Assiah, as the Daughter or second Hé, to Malkuth. In this plan "Kether" seems to have no place. Again, sometimes the whole "Tree" is considered as if it were represented on Four Planes, one above the other, or interpenetrating each other. In this case we get 40 Sephiroth, Ten for each World; and for purposes of classification each Sephira was considered to contain another complete tree, so as to make in all 400, with a correspondingly great number of paths. This plan seems to have been little used for practical purposes; it is, of course, very complicated and difficult to conceive on Four Planes at the same time.

The only other attempt, that I am aware of, was to place the Diagram of one Tree above the other, so that the Kether of the Lowest touched the Malkuth of the next, and so on with the other two higher Worlds. Such an arrangement is shown in Mathers "Kaballah Unveiled," where the Influences from the Archetypal World are shown descending, by means of arrows running along the Paths of the Flaming Sword (but, be it noted, there is no connecting path from Binah to Chesed on the Tree), and then through the Creative and Formative Worlds to Assiah, where the current ended in Malkuth of the Lowest Tree.

But no one seems to have shown a LIVING TREE with Its Roots in the Infinitely Small and its Branches spreading out to the Infinitely Great. Yet it is called the TREE OF LIFE. It would seem, in the past, it has been little better than the Tree of the Knowledge of Good and Evil.

One can only account for Attainment by the Old System, as by the Grace of God. The "Paths" wrongly arranged (but the Sephiroth—corresponding to the Grades—fortunately in perfect Order) were confusing rather than illuminating; the method of progress leading to the Horrors of "The Abyss" between Chesed and Binah. However, that makes little difference if my surmise is correct (as explained in the "Egyptian Revival") that during this Aeon, Wisdom and Understanding are directly projected upon the Children of Earth, and the Abyss definitely Bridged.

But to return to the further development of this wonderful Plan. On Monday, April 16th, I had occasion to visit a friend and Brother, who is a cunning craftsman and

THE BODY OF GOD

designer. He is a man of much intelligence, but not a deep Student of the Qabalah, his interest in this matter having dated from a cursory reading of "The Essence of the Practical Qabalah" followed by some study of "Q.B.L." a few weeks ago. I was impressed to ask his opinion of the New Plan, and found that he grasped its possibilities at once. We discussed it for some time and made a temporary sketch similar to the one I first drew (Fig. XXI). He offered to make me a careful drawing showing several progressions.

The following day I called upon him again, when we made some further experiments together, and discussed the proper proportion of the Diameters of the Sephiroth in their relation to the Paths. It was noticed that the Paths from Chesed to Tiphereth, and from Geburah to Tiphereth, would generate a similar "Tree" between Tiphereth and Yesod in addition to the one between Yesod and Malkuth. Then he was illuminated by the Idea that an intermediate "Tree" extending from the Centre of Tiphereth to the Centre of Malkuth should be formed, and another one half the size, between the Centre of Yesod and the Centre of Malkuth. This Idea produced startling results. The Second Tree was exactly Half the Height of the First, and the Third, Half that of the Second (perfect octaves).[1] The Size of the

---

[1] "Architecture is frozen music," is the saying of Frederich Schlegel. And if this saying is anywhere significant surely it is so in relation to polyphonic music and Gothic architecture. In each there is the progressive playing of part against part, the building up of member against member, each structure completed only to point to a still incomplete superstructure, joining in the endless aspirational upward sweep of the whole. Arch rests upon arch, flying buttress upon buttress, pinnacle rises above pinnacle,—everywhere there is a balance not quite attained, a symmetry not quite perfected,—and by and by we realize that no Gothic church can ever be *completed;* its beauty is its eternal promise, its endless upward flight. Is not this the very image of contrapuntal music, and of its supreme expression in the fugue?" Hartley Burr Alexander, Nature and Human Nature.

Sephiroth should progress accordingly, and be based upon the original generating Circles of the whole Tree. It was then found that the Kether of the Second was in the Centre of the Tiphereth of the First, and its Tiphereth in the Yesod of the First, while its Malkuth was in the First Malkuth.

The Third "Tree" had its Kether in the Yesod of the First, and the Tiphereth of the Second; while its Malkuth was again in the Centre of the Malkuth of Both. In other words the CENTRE of MALKUTH represented the INFINITELY SMALL, and the Triple Trees went on Increasing in Size by octaves to Infinity, while MALKUTH continued to EXPAND about its OWN CENTRE.

The accompanying Plate will show this marvelous Plan in great clearness of detail.

At this point we must clearly realize that since the Plan of the Thirty-two Paths of Wisdom is ever increasing in orderly progression towards the Infinitely Great, or Nuit, and at the same time contracting in the same proportions towards the Infinitely Small, or Hadit, the Concealed Father of All, it is no longer proper for us to talk of the Influence as ascending or descending. But, since the extremely minute is more quickly lost to view, and on account of the inconvenience and difficulty of making a drawing of a very small size, we must start from a Central Point in Malkuth, and discuss the subject as if the "Tree" were increasing in size from that Point.

Thus, for convenience, we shall now call the smallest visible Tree in our Design, the First, the next larger, the Second, and so on for the necessary number of progressions.

The Central Dot in Malkuth of the First Tree represents Hadit. This should be considered as an unextended Point of Light or Pure Essence of Being, the true comple-

THE BODY OF GOD

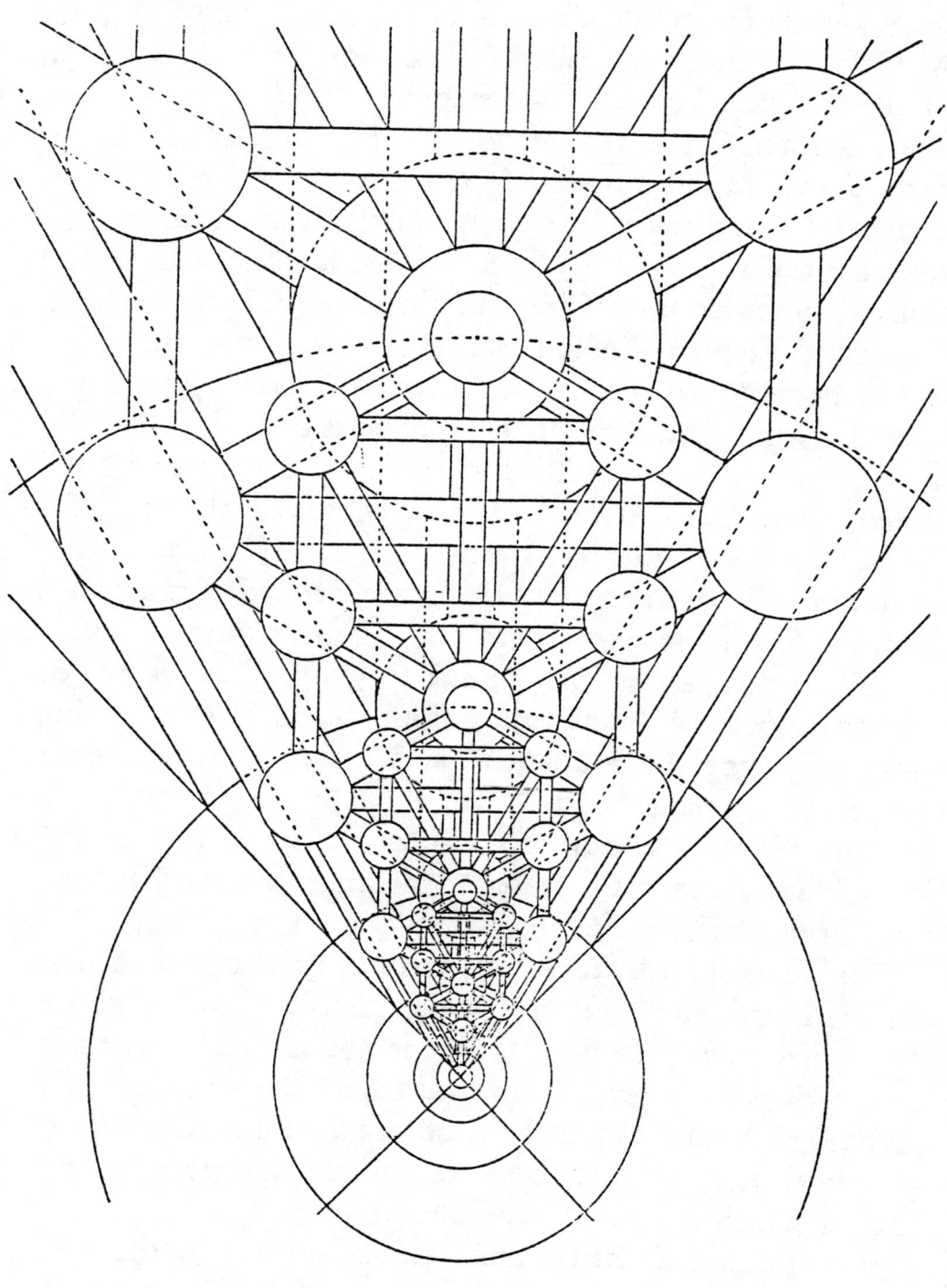

PLATE A

ment of the Infinitely Great and unknown Body of Nuit which is beyond our utmost conception of the expansion of the Greatest Tree we can imagine.

The small Circle around this "Point" is Malkuth of the First Tree, and the Tree itself may, for convenience, be considered as *growing up out of Malkuth,* just like any other tree in proper soil. The *True Kether* is concealed within this as the Essence of Life and Form is within the Seed. When we reach the "Manifested Kether" of the First Tree it will be very much like *the most perfect fruit* containing within it the "seed" of further progression.

We have been accustomed to consider the "Tree of Life" as *descending from Kether,* but now that we realize that the "Tree" grows to Infinity, we cannot conceive of a starting point at the Top, so as to work downwards. We must start from the Centre and work outwards and upwards.

It will not be possible for me to give all the details of this marvelous plan, but I may point out a few interesting features, leaving the Student to add the results of his own researches, as time goes on.

I am of course adopting the "Reformulated Plan of the Paths," but some may prefer to arrange them otherwise; it makes no difference to the general geometrical design.

The Correspondences and Attributions of the First Tree will therefore remain exactly the same as previously given. Each aspirant will have to fulfill the necessary requirements of mastering the "Ideas" connected therewith, as before. He will have to Attain, as formerly, before the Fuller Consciousness comes to him; but there are additional "clues" to his progress which are most valuable.

For instance: If he commences his Journey by the Path of Aleph, the Pure Fool, leading from Malkuth to Yesod,

THE BODY OF GOD

when he has traveled *half-way* up this Path, he will obtain an additional influx of Power from the corresponding Path on the *Second Tree*. He will have reached the circumference of the *Second Malkuth*. On arrival in Yesod, he will have contacted the circumference of *Malkuth of the Third Tree*.

Let us consider his progress up the Central Pillar first; supposing it to be possible for him thus to travel in perfect equilibrium from the start.

On the Path of Mem or "The Hanged Man," which is attributed to "Water," he will receive the additional Power of the "Air" from the Path of Aleph in the *Second Tree*, till he reaches the First Tiphereth. That is to say, for instance, he will find a *greater use* for Pranayama; and so on. But before he enters Tiphereth he will already be receiving the benefit of the Influence of the *Yesod* of the *Second Tree*, which he will have contacted after crossing the Reciprocal Path of "The Hierophant" or Taurus. All the way from the First Yesod to "The Abyss" he will be receiving the still higher power of Aleph of the *Third Tree*.

As he begins his ascent from the First Tiphereth he will do so by the Path of "Shin" or "The Great Judgment." This is the Way of the Triple Spirit and of Fire, but thereon he will also feel the influence of "The Hanged Man" from the *Second Tree*, as well as from "The Fool" of the *Third*.

On crossing the "Path of Death" he will leave behind him the influence of *Yesod* of the *Second Tree*, but half-way across the Abyss he will contact the Influence of the "Hierophant" of the *Second*, and at the same moment enter the sphere of *Yesod of the Third Tree*.

Next, he will cross the Path of the "Star" or Aquarius, on the primary Tree, contacting immediately the *Tiphereth* of Tree *Number Two*, through the aura of which he passes on to the *First Kether Attainment*.

During this Journey up the Central Pillar, his original Malkuth will have doubled in diameter on the Path of Aleph, doubled again when he reached Yesod, again on reaching Tiphereth, and once more on his attainment to Kether, which then Crowns his Work.

Thus the First Kether Attainment is representative of the Fifth Visible Progression of the Sphere of Malkuth, after which the Aspirant begins to contact the Sixth progression of the Whole Tree, and from that point in his Career, every further progression of Malkuth will touch the centre of a Higher Kether, to Infinity. But as the Sixth visible Progression of Malkuth contacts the Second visible Kether; the Seventh, the Third; and so on, there will always seem to be Four untraveled Trees between. It may be that these represent the "Four Worlds" of the Qabalah, and that he must in reality always progress in the Four Worlds simultaneously.

It will be noticed that the Path of Beth, or Wisdom, leading from the first Malkuth to Hod, the Sphere of Mercury, contains, essentially, all the Powers of Mercury or "The Magician" to Infinity in that direction; since this Path leads to larger and larger "Hods" in regular sequence.

Similarly, the Path of Daleth or Love, "The Empress," or Venus, leading to Netzach, continues to Infinity in that direction also. So we find all Love and Wisdom concentrated in the centre of Malkuth. Since all the "Three Mothers," Aleph, Mem, and Shin, interblend on the Middle Pillar, these Powers are also fully concentrated in the Centre of Malkuth, and conversely, proceed from It.

In regard to the other Paths and Sephiroth of the First Tree—and this applies equally to All the Trees—we may

THE BODY OF GOD

point out that Netzach and Hod will always be found in the exact Centres of the Paths of Venus and Mercury on the next larger Tree.

Chesed and Geburah are always exactly in the Centres of the Paths of Cancer, "The Chariot," and Luna, "The High-Priestess," of the next larger Tree.

Chokmah and Binah will always have their Centres in Leo, the path of "Strength" and Gemini, or "The Lovers," of the next progressed Tree.

Kether always appears in the Centre of the *next* Tiphereth, and of the *following* Yesod, to infinity. In other words, the Light is always within the Life of the Sun, and the Sun within the Body of the Moon.

The Reciprocal Path of "The Hierophant" will always have an influence horizontally across the Abyss of the next Tree below. The path of the "Hanged Man" will always leave Him suspended from the Reciprocal path of "The Star" or Aquarius of the "next" tree, while he is seen below Tiphereth on his own Tree. This is exactly where he is mystically *supposed to be* according to the old system of paths, although he was otherwise *assigned*.

It is a matter of almost unending interest to trace out these various combinations, but there are even more important considerations ahead of us. We must leave the Student to work things out in his own way, and pass on to wider fields of study.

CHAPTER VI

DURING the afternoon of April 17th, after obtaining a glimpse of the foregoing possibilities while discussing the details of this Plan, a still wider conception dawned upon me.

Since the Centre of Malkuth has become the Point from which All proceeds, why should the Tree grow only in one Direction?

What we have been calling the "lower" part of the Tree is in the form of an Equilateral Triangle, and the Progression of the Trees only increases the size of this indefinitely. Surely there must be *Six* such Trees, forming a Star, and so filling every direction of two-dimensional space.

This seemed to throw light on some little understood passages of the "Sepher Yetzirah," which I shall now further quote. It will be remembered that the last words we studied in that connection were: *"These Ten Numbers, beyond the universal One, have the boundless realms, boundless origin and end,"* but the verse goes on: *"an abyss of good and one of evil, boundless height and depth, East and West, North and South, and the one only God and King, faithful for ever seated on his throne, shall rule over all, for ever and ever."*

This is striking evidence that our Plan is that which was intended to be conveyed by the Author of this mysterious treatise. I may now quote the remaining verses in the First Chapter, since these make the matter still clearer.

THE BODY OF GOD

"These ten Sephiroth which are ineffable, whose appearance is like scintillating flames, have no end, but are infinite. The word of God is in them as they burst forth, and as they return; they obey the divine command, rushing along as a whirlwind, and returning to prostrate themselves at his throne."

This seems fairly understandable in the Light of the Two Infinites with the manifested Universe, Ever-Becoming, between Them.

"These ten Sephiroth which are, moreover, ineffable, have their end even as their beginning, conjoined, even as is a flame to a burning coal: for our God is superlative in his unity, and does not permit any second one. And who canst thou place before the only one?"

In other words: Nuit, Hadit, Ra-Hoor-Khuit, are a Perfect Three in One.

"And as to this Decad of the Sephiroth, restrain thy lips from comment, and thy mind from thought of them, and if thy heart fail thee, return to thy place; therefore is it written 'The living creatures ran and returned,' and on this wise was the covenant made with us."

This means that since the "Tree" is everywhere the same in every part of space, once its general attributions are fixed in the mind, it is not well to confuse ourselves by too much attempt at progressed expansion of the idea. Rather we should return and contemplate the Centre from which All proceeds, thus obtaining the Pure Essence Here and Now.

"These are the ten emanations of number. One is the Spirit of the Living God, blessed and more than blessed be the name of the Living God of the Ages. The Holy Spirit is his Voice, his Spirit, and his Word."

This is very similar to the instruction in Liber Legis:

"Be thou Hadit my secret centre, my heart and my tongue," but CCXX is a new Covenant, and goes much further than the old one recorded in the Sepher Yetzirah.

Second, from the Spirit be made Air and formed for speech, twenty-two letters, three of which are mothers, A, M, Sh; seven are double, B, G, D, K, P, R, Th; and twelve are single, E, V, Z, Ch, T, I, L, N, S, O, Tz, Q; but the spirit is first among these. Third, PRIMITIVE WATER HE ALSO FORMED AND DESIGNED FROM HIS SPIRIT,[1] *and from the void and formless made earth even as a rampart, or standing wall, and* VARIED ITS SURFACE AS THE CROSSING OF BEAMS. *Fourth, from the Water, He designed Fire, and from it formed to himself a throne of honour, with Auphanim, Seraphim, Holy Animals, and ministering Angels, and with these he formed his dwelling, as it is written in the text 'Who makest his angels spirits and his ministers a flaming fire.' (Psalm 104, v. 4.)"*

Note the reference to the design made from Primitive Water by the Spirit, and also about the "crossed beams" or Paths of the Tree. His thrones of Honour are the Manifested Kethers. Holy animals refer to Zodiac, etc.

"He selected three letters from the simple ones, and sealed them as forming his great Name IHU *and he sealed the universe in* SIX DIRECTIONS.

---

[1] Since writing the above, a new literal translation of the Sepher Yetzirah, by Mr. Knut Stenring, has appeared. I quote a part of his rendering of the above verse, since it includes a reference of great importance to the theory in hand: "Three—Water from Air: He wrote and formed therein twenty-two letters, from the formless and void—mire and clay; He designed them as a platband, He hewed them as a wall, He covered them as a building. *He poured snow over them and it became earth, even as it is written: 'He saith to the snow: Be thou the earth'* (Job xxxvii. 6)."

This reference to *snow* is quite startling in light of what follows in the present treatise.

THE BODY OF GOD 53

PLATE B
THE MACROCOSMIC SNOWFLAKE

Five. He looked above, and sealed the height, with IHU.
Six. He looked below, and sealed the deep, with IUH.
Seven. He looked forward, and sealed the East, with HIU.
Eight. He looked backward, and sealed the West, with UHI.
Nine. He looked to the right, and sealed the South, with UIH.
Ten. He looked to the left, and sealed the North, with HUI.
"These are the ten ineffable existences, the Spirit of the Living God, Air, Water, Fire, Height and Depth, East and West, North and South."

So ends the first Chapter of this mysterious treatise, and there is little doubt that our Six-fold Star is the solution of the problem which has puzzled the Qabalists for so many Centuries. With its Centre it forms the Heptad.

Let us now examine the Design of this wonderful new Star, as drawn in such minute detail. (See Plate B.)

A glorious vista opens before us—Infinite Space in the Form of a *Pure Snow Flake*. What could be a better way of "Fixing the Design in its Purity"? What more likely, since all things are said to have proceeded from the Primal Water under the action of Spirit, than that the Substance should Crystallize in *exactly the same way* that any drop of water, or any crystal, is found to take form under the direction of the lines of polar force which always form six radiating lines or axes in every rain drop which becomes a snow-flake?

Surely this is a pure enough conception of the beginning of all things and the infinite progression of this manifested Universe. Scientifically it can hardly be denied.

THE BODY OF GOD

Thus the Pure Essence of the Soul of Man may also crystallize and become a Centre of the Great Star. This may take place at any point in space and at any moment in time, for the Centre of the Infinite is Everywhere and the Circumference Nowhere.

What a vista of Attainment opens up before every human being, for we have been told in Liber Legis: "Every man and every woman is a star." Also "Every number is infinite; there is no difference."

But let us consider a few more details of this Divine Plan. What changes have really occurred owing to our Multiplication of the Stone of the Wise?

Netzach and Hod and the Paths of Venus and Mercury —which before were seen to progress directly to infinity— have now *become forever united*. There is no difference; *Love is ever under Will*.

Again, these Combined Paths are exactly equal to the Paths of Aleph, Mem and Shin which formed the equilibrated Middle Pillar, for the Father and Mother together equal the Child. *Every Path* radiating from the Centre is now Equilibrated or Balanced.

The combined Sphere of Netzach-Hod or Venus-Mercury is always to be found exactly between the Spheres of Binah and Chokmah of the Two Trees of the Scale below. Also the combined Paths of Venus-Mercury always lie exactly between the Spheres of Chesed and Geburah, or Mercy and Severity of the "Tree" below, and so on to Infinity.

All else remains the same, but there is no longer any possibility of unbalanced progress.

But we must not forget the instruction in Liber Legis, which is of the utmost importance."The Khabs is in the Khu, not the Khu in the Khabs. Worship then the Khabs and behold my light shed over you!" We must Worship the Central Point which is concealed in Malkuth and in the Centre of our Being; then only will the True Light of Infinity be shed upon us. If we fail in this, seeking in the outer, our minds fall back, failing to grasp that which is beyond our finite vision. "The Living Creatures run and return" and having returned, the Illusions of Space and Time are exchanged for the Everpresent Here and Now. The Introduction to this treatise should now be more clearly understandable to the average reader. We can see how the Light or Fruit of Light, the Six Kethers, are always First in Advance towards the Infinite without. Next follows the progress of the Life or Soul of Nature and of Man, then follows the regular progression of the Sphere of Malkuth in ever-widening Circles as "Matter" eats up "Form" and the "Form" comprehends the Efficient Cause, which is itself the manifestation of the Invisible Final Cause.

But Malkuth is also Nuit, for "Matter" or "Substance" is continuous, so it is equally true to say that She contracts upon Hadit the Invisible Centre, or that He Expands towards Her Infinite Girth. Ra-Hoor-Khuit, with His twin Hoor-Pa-Kraat hidden within Him, may be called Heru-Ra-Ha as the Crowned Child, the whole Manifest Universe in Time and Space, which is the Star 418.

This, too, is the Great Hexagram of the Macrocosm, but what of the Pentagram, the Microcosm, MAN?

Another great Mystery lies before us, needing only to be Brought to Light, as will be shown in the next Chapter.

CHAPTER VII

WE HAVE seen in the last Chapter how our original conception of "The Tree of Life" may be multiplied and crystallized into a Macrocosmic Snow Flake, or Six-fold Star. Let us now return to our first simple form of the "Tree" and examine it more carefully with a view to further discoveries.

We have been accustomed to look upon this as representing a flat two-dimensional surface, but we were not necessarily correct in our supposition.

In reality we have been looking at the front surface of a *Triangular Crystal Prism*,[1] and what we saw was *not all in one plane*. The "sides" of the Tree are but two angles of an equilateral solid; the third angle, at the back, is invisible, being completely hidden by the Paths of the Central Pillar.

This Central Pillar is not level with the front surface, but is the *Core* of the prism. Kether is the Apex of a Pyramid whose base is equilateral. Malkuth is at the lower point of a descending pyramid, all four sides of which are equilateral, thus forming a Tetrahedron.

---

[1] Chaos or Matter is potentially a prism which refracts the great Light-Source, splitting up the Supernal Light into stars, or the Supreme Consciousness into Ideas. As matter or substance becomes organized and develops mind, its power as a prism grows. As we clarify our minds they become as living, organic prisms which act with increasing precision and detail. The more definite and authentic our ideas, the more accurate and mathematical, the more will they focus Light from the Supreme, till 'sleeping stars' slip on their livery of light. The more exact the form, the closer the correspondence between the Son (or Form, Prism, Expression, Becoming) and the Father (or Light, Life, Love, Understanding).—J. S. Forrester-Brown, "The Two Creation Stories."

Tiphereth and Yesod are both embedded in the solid, and the Paths of the "Three Mothers" are *interior* channels.

Looking at the "Tree" in the ordinary manner, we should have to realize that only the Three Reciprocal Paths, and the Four Paths forming the Side Pillars, are actually on the level surface before us. There are, however, three Reciprocal Paths of each kind, viz.: nine in all, for there are two others, in each case, which retreat and meet at the third angle of the prism. There is another pair of vertical Paths, similar to those at the sides, but concealed at the back of the solid.

Instead of there being only two Paths from Kether to Chokmah and Binah, there are *three*, one sloping away to the concealed angle at the back. The triangular surface we see is not vertical, but *slopes back* towards Kether.

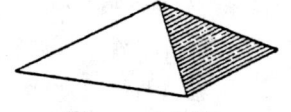

Figure XXIII

The Paths from Chokmah and Binah to Tiphereth also slope inward to the central core of the prism, and there is a third Path from the angle at the back.

The four visible Paths from Chesed, Geburah, Netzach, and Hod to Tiphereth, are likewise sloping within the solid and there are in addition two invisible Paths at the back.

The Paths from Netzach and Hod to Yesod also incline inward, since Yesod is at the core of the Tree. Again there is another similar Path concealed, which slopes down from the angle at the back.

The surface of the Triangle formed by the Paths connecting Netzach, Hod and Malkuth, is not vertical, but falls

THE BODY OF GOD

away towards the back, and there are two similar surfaces connected with the concealed Sphere of Netzach-Hod behind the solid figure.

This, at first, may seem confusing, but it can be more clearly explained by means of diagrams and plates.

Let us imagine that we have ascended above the Tree and are looking directly down upon Kether. From this position we should perceive a triangular figure as shown in the diagram:

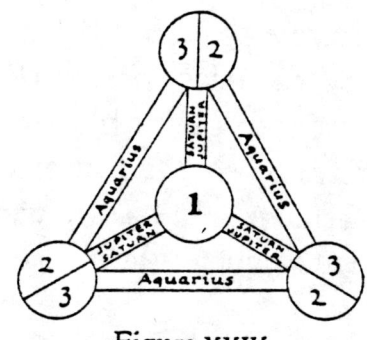

Figure XXIV

The nearest point to us will be Kether and the other three Spheres at a lower level. The three triangular surfaces slope away from Kether to the Spheres at the angles.

But what are these Three Spheres and Six Paths, upon which we have been looking? Our conception of the Tree must undergo a remarkable change. The Three bounding Paths are all equally that of Tzaddi, Aquarius, or "The Star." The Three Spheres are each equally both Chokmah and Binah. The Three Paths connecting with Kether are each equally Jupiter and Saturn, or Kaph and Tau, or "The Wheel" and "The Universe." In other words, THERE ARE NO LONGER ANY PAIRS OF OPPOSITES, and there never were in reality. Each idea is only true insofar as it contains its own opposite. So the Sphere we called Chokmah has always concealed its Binah, and Binah its Chokmah, and so on. While we thought the Tree represented a flat surface we could not realize how these apparently opposite Spheres could in reality be one and the same, but now that we have discovered the Third Angle of the Prism, they are at once unified without difficulty.

Also the former Reciprocal Paths have now become the Boundaries of the Solid Figure, and represent a sectional Plane through it. The natures of the opposite Paths are also unified, and they convey the Single Influence of Kether to the Dual Spheres they connect therewith.

Let us now include Tiphereth in our conception, and at the same time imagine that we are looking at the solid from the front, but that it has been twisted round slightly, so as to make the concealed angle clearer.

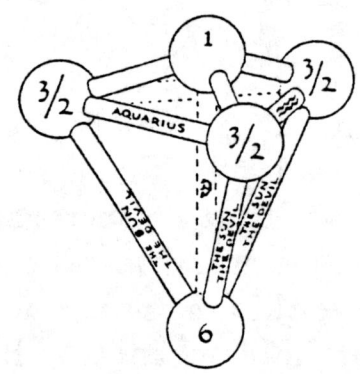

Figure XXV

We now see how the Paths of Resh and Ayin or "The Sun" and "The Devil," are *triple*, yet *one*. These conflicting ideas have disappeared in a harmonious combination. The Path of Shin, the Holy Spirit, at the core of the Figure uniting Kether and Tiphereth, remains single.

THE BODY OF GOD

What were the Pillars of Mercy and Severity, are now no longer opposed to one another, for there are Three bounding Pillars, as well as the Central One.

There are Three Chesed-Geburahs, and Three Netzach-Hods. The Paths of Sameck and Pé, or "Temperance" and "The Tower," are now united, as are those of Lamed and Yod, or "Justice" and "The Hermit."

If we were next to take a section through the "Tree" at the Line formed by the Path of Nun, or "Death," and remove the upper portion, while *looking down* upon the remainder we should see:

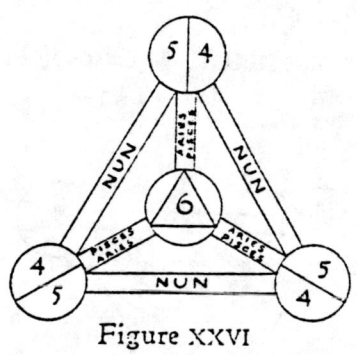

Figure XXVI

The bounding lines, nearest to us, would be the Three Paths of Nun with the Three Spheres of Chesed-Geburah at the angles. Tiphereth would be somewhat lower down, and the Three Paths of Hé-Qoph, or Aries-Pisces, would slope towards it. The small triangle near the centre would be the lower part of the three paths of the Resh-Ayin triad.

If we next cut through the prism at the Path of Vau, or "The Hierophant" while still *looking down* at the remainder, we should see:

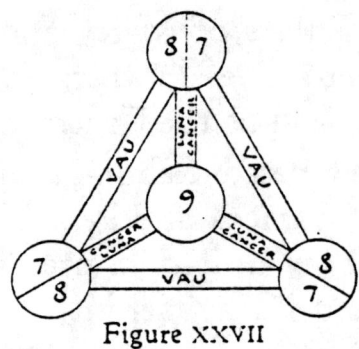

Figure XXVII

Yesod in the Centre, somewhat below the bounding lines and Spheres of the triple paths of Vau and the three Netzach-Hods. In this instance there would be no small triad in the centre, since there are no paths equivalent to those mentioned in regard to the upper section.

But if from this position we looked *up* at the section above we should see:

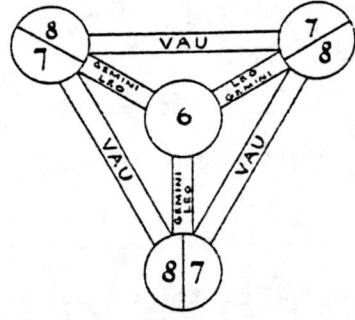

Figure XXVIII

The same Spheres and Paths bounding the figure, but Tiphereth would appear in the centre, connected by the triple Paths of Teth-Zain, or "The Lion-Lovers," corresponding to Leo-Gemini.

Finally, should we look *up* at the whole Tree from below Malkuth, we should perceive:

THE BODY OF GOD 63

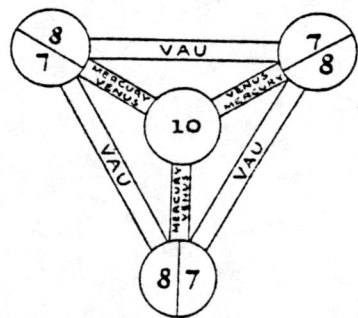

Figure XXIX

Malkuth in the Centre, nearest to us, with the Triple Path, or Plane, of the "Hierophant" some distance above. These would be connected by the triple Paths of Beth-Daleth, Mercury-Venus, or "The Magician-Empress."

Thus, in every instance, would the "pairs of opposites" be truly mated and resolved into a unified triplicity, in three dimensions.

The accompanying Plate shows the whole "Prismatic Tree" with its 13 Spheres and 36 Paths, quite clearly. The whole number is 49, which again returns to Unity as 13. 49 also represents the square of seven, and the Hebrew Word for "Solvé." (See plate "C" and study carefully.)

We may now consider approximately what would be the impression received by one who took an "Astral Journey" up through the Central Core of this Triple Tree.

Starting from Malkuth by the Path of Aleph, or The Fool, the astral form would travel vertically upwards, with a consciousness of being surrounded by the combined influences of Mercury-Venus perfectly blended, while the surrounding "space" would take the form of an ever-increasing triangle, till Yesod was reached. At this juncture he would feel the *concentrated* essence of the forces from the Paths

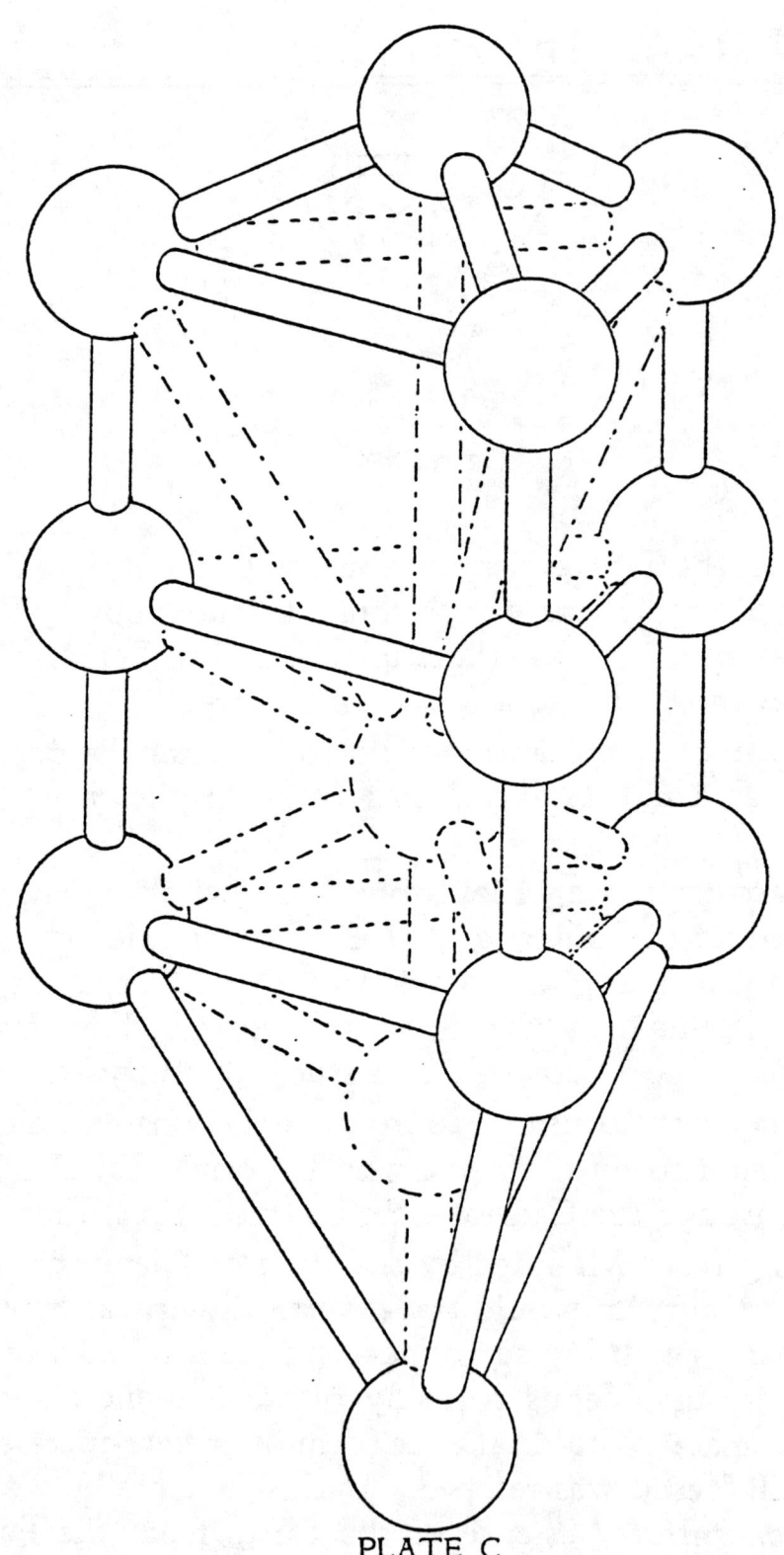

PLATE C

THE BODY OF GOD

of Cancer-Luna (The "Chariot-High Priestess" or Pure Balanced Aspiration) while yet his consciousness continued to expand till he reached the full limits of the equilateral triangle bounded by the paths of "The Hierophant." From Yesod onward to this point he would partake of the Mystery of the "Hanged-Man" (Primitive Water) till the Influence of the Hierophantic Plane began to initiate him into its deeper Meanings. As he continued by this Path of Mem his field of consciousness would remain extended to its limits, held there by the Forces of Yod-Lamed or "The Hermit and Justice," while, at the same time, there would be a contraction due to the influence of the Triple Paths of Zain-Teth which would concentrate his Soul in Tiphereth.

Rising above Tiphereth his Soul would expand to the limits of his field of consciousness by means of the Paths of Hé-Qoph (or Aries-Pisces), while he would also have contacted the Influence of the Holy Spirit in the Central Path of Shin. This would expand within the Soul, under the influence of the triple Paths of Ayin-Resh (or Capricorn-Sol). Passing through the Plane of "Death" or Scorpio, he would ascend till his Spiritual Consciousness expanded to the limits of his Soul Consciousness, which would have been affected, meanwhile, by the Paths of Pé-Samech or Mars-Sagittarius ("The Tower-Temperance") and presently he would reach the Plane of "The Star" (Tzaddi or Aquarius) where his Soular and Spiritual Fields of Consciousness would be equally extended, while the Spirit would steadily Flame in the Core of his Being.

Then, after contacting the Triple Influence of Chokmah-Binah, his whole Field of Consciousness, on all Planes, would gradually contract along the Paths of Kaph-Tau upon Kether, upon reaching which, he would suddenly find

Himself once more in *Malkuth*, which is the Body of Nuit, concentrated upon the Inner Light of the Khabs, the only veil of Hadit, the Flame in every Heart of Man and in the Core of every Star.

He would then arise as a truly Enlightened Being, clothed in a body of Flesh, ready to go forth and do his pleasure among the living. As it is written in the Ritual of Mercury: "I travel upon high, I tread upon the Firmament of Nu, I raise a flashing-flame with the Lightning of Mine Eye; ever rushing on in the Splendour of the daily Glorified Ra; giving my life to the dwellers of Earth."

Truly will he have learned the meaning of 49, which is Solvé.

CHAPTER VIII

AVING briefly discussed the "Tree of Life" in its Prismatic form, we should now pass on to a consideration of its "Multiplication" and "Projection"; for we have indeed found it to be "The Stone of the Wise."

This Crystal Stone is capable of indefinite increase or decrease, very much in the same manner as was found possible in regard to the flat two-dimensional figure.

The Centre of Malkuth will once more be our starting point, and now we shall find the *smallest* Tree will be *within* the next larger one, and so on. (See Plate D.)

The Central Core of this Prismatic Tree will always consist of Malkuth, Yesod, Tiphereth and Kether, united by the Three Channels of Aleph, Mem, and Shin. These will be found to combine and recombine as the "Tree" progresses in size. The Kether of the smallest Tree will always be embedded in the Tiphereth of the next larger, and these two again in the Yesod of the next. The triplication of the Tree makes little difference to these Sephiroth and Paths, but we shall find it affects some of the others.

The Three Netzach-Hods of the smallest Tree will appear as *spheres* in the centre of the Three Venus-Mercury Paths of the next larger, and so on, indefinitely.

The Three Chesed-Geburahs of the smallest Tree will form similar spheres in the centres of the Triple Channels of Cancer-Luna of the next Tree.

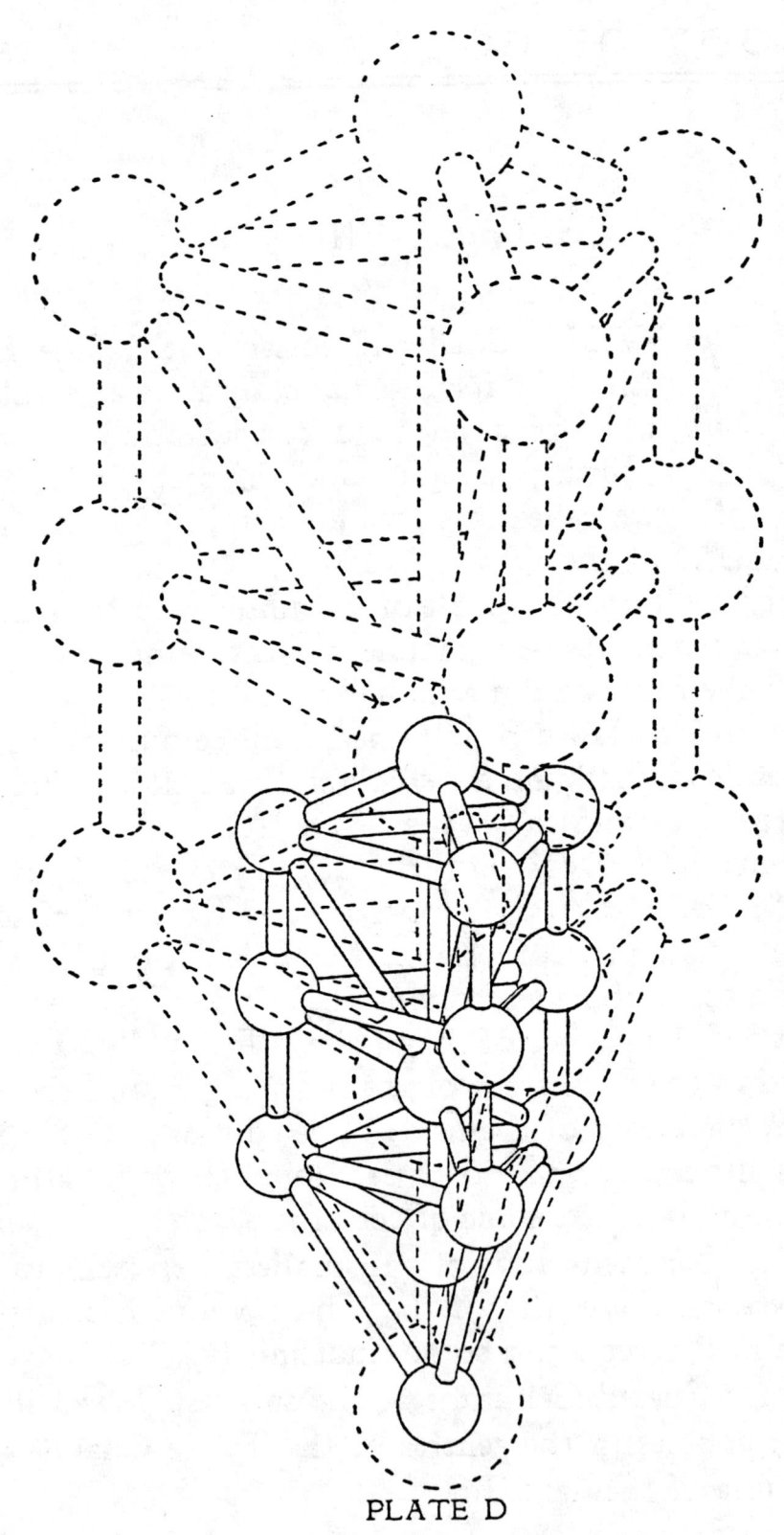

PLATE D

THE BODY OF GOD

The Three Chokmah-Binahs will likewise be found in the centres of the Three Channels of Leo-Gemini, and so on. These last named spheres will always be half way embedded in the surface of the Sphere of Yesod of the next larger Prismatic Tree.

The Student should trace out these correspondences for himself, making a careful study of the accompanying Plate D, while endeavoring to form a complete mental picture of these Prismatic Trees.

We are now prepared to take another step in the development of this marvelous Plan, but first let us return for a moment to the contemplation of the design of our "Crystalline Snow-Flake" as shown in Plate B.

In dealing with the two-dimensional aspect of the Work, we found upon combining SIX of the flat "Trees" we obtained a Hexagonal Figure or *Sixfold-Star*. This symbolism is that of the Macrocosm. What will be the result of our combining a number of the solid Prismatic Trees?

Upon experiment we find in this instance that they do not combine in six-fold arrangement as before, but that FIVE such Prisms taken together form a perfect *Pentagon*, the centre of which is Malkuth and the bounding lines all representing the Paths of Taurus or "The Hierophant." The lines connecting the Spheres at the five angles, which are all Netzach-Hods, will each be Paths of Venus-Mercury.

Of course, looking at the solid figure from this angle, Malkuth is *nearer to us* than the Netzach-Hod Spheres, for the latter are connected by the retreating Paths of Venus-Mercury. In addition to this Pentagon we should also see something of the remainder of the five solid Trees, in perspective, as they spread out behind or away from us.

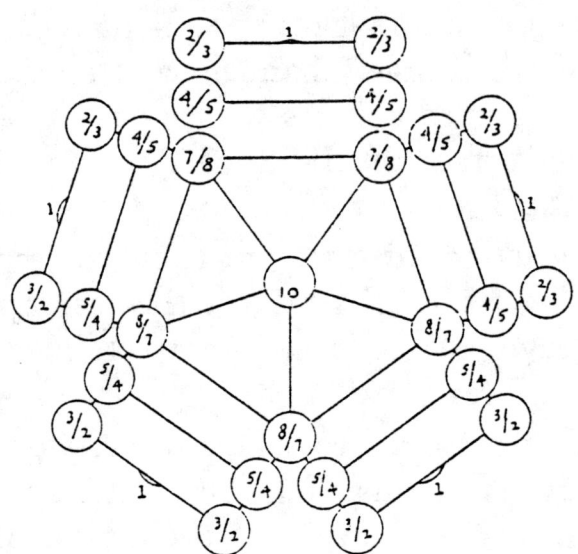

Figure XXX

The Great Work, as symbolized in the Word of the Aeon, ABRAHADABRA, has always consisted in finding the equivalence between the Microcosm and the Macrocosm, or the formula 5° = 6°. Here we find a higher aspect of that Work, for this solid Figure is built up on purely Microcosmic Lines of Five Solids to a section. But we have now discovered a "Rose"[1] capable of extension in Five Directions to Infinity, and containing within itself all the Correspondences, with powers of indefinite multiplication.

Such a figure is not capable of filling the whole of Space, but when we take FOUR such sections and combine them,

---

[1] Here, of course, the "Mystic Rose" is referred to, but since writing the above an interesting passage from Dr. Oken's work "Abriss der Naturphilosophye" Gottingen 1805, has been brought to my attention. He writes, page 65, —on the whole all plants are only metamorphoses of the Syngenesis. Here is united, what in the others is only blossoming disconnectedly. The importance of the number *five*, so unchangeably sacred to *plants*, will yet have to find its solution in the Mathesis; *without any doubt it lies hidden under the Dodecahedron consisting of Pentagrams, as the crystalized sphere.*" This is startling confirmation of what followed upon my own researches. Achad.

THE BODY OF GOD 71

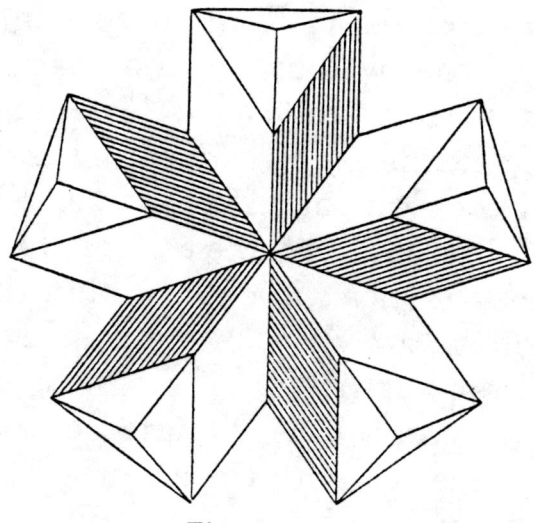

Figure XXXI

we are able to make a Complete Three Dimensional Solid, which will extend in every direction as the Trees Progress in Size, thus completely filling all known space. Such a figure is composed of Twenty of our original Prismatic Trees, and 20 is the Numeration of IVD, the basic letter of the Hebrew Alphabet, and the First letter of the Ineffable Name. It is also the Numeration of the Letter Kaph, which corresponds to "The Wheel of Life" and the Father Iu-Pater.

When these are so combined, the central Point of Malkuth is completely embedded in the Centre of the Figure (unless it be built of actual Crystals, in which case we should be able to get a glimpse of it).

The accompanying plate showing the "Projection" of the Stone, will make the matter clear to the Student, and open up a wonderful vista to his mind.

We have now a figure capable of progression in twenty directions. The true Kether is concealed within the Malkuth at the Centre, and this expands spherically as the size of the solid increases.

We have 20 Projecting Kethers representing the Forerunners of Light, followed by 60 Chokmah-Binahs and 60 Chesed-Geburahs. Then follow 20 Tiphereths concealed in the cores of the Prisms and representing the Substance of Light which is the Soul or Life. We are able to perceive only 12 Netzach-Hods, for these have now united into groups of five dual spheres in one. Within the cores of the prisms, next follow 20 Yesods, while a single Malkuth is at the Central Point of All.

We have, therefore, One Hundred and Ninety-Three Spheres in all, connected with the un-progressed figure, and this number reduces to Thirteen, which is UNITY. 193, it may be remarked, is also a prime number.

There are 60 Paths equivalent to Iu-Pater-Saturn; 60 which correspond to Aquarius; 60 to Sagittarius-Mars; 60 to Scorpio; and 60 to Libra-Virgo.

But there are only 30 representing Taurus or "The Hierophant" since these have now combined in pairs.

Thus, we have 330 Visible Paths.

There are 20 Invisible Paths of Air.
        20 Invisible Paths of Water.
        20 Invisible Paths of Fire or Spirit.
        60 Invisible Paths of Sol-Capricorn.
        60 Invisible Paths of Leo-Gemini.
        60 Invisible Paths of Cancer-Luna.

But only 12 Invisible Paths of Venus-Mercury.

Thus we have 252 Invisible Paths in all. The Paths of the Tree were always attributed to The Serpent; it is strange that these invisible Paths should be 252, which is the numeration of the Hebrew word MAVRH, meaning "The Serpent's Den."

The Total number of Paths in the complete figure is

THE BODY OF GOD

PLATE E

THE GARDEN OF EDEN

This represents the *First* or simple prismatic "Tree" branching out in 20 directions from its Central Malkuth. It should be observed that if the *Second* progression of the solid be taken as far as Tiphereth. it would exactly enclose this in a perfect Dodecahedron comprising 20 solid angles forming 12 equilateral Pentagons: while the *Fifth* progression of the original Malkuth would exactly enclose all this in a perfect Sphere.

thus 330 plus 252 which is 582. 330, the number of visible Paths is equivalent to the Hebrew word MTzR meaning: Boundary, Terminus, or Crosspath. 582 reduces to 15, the numeration of IH the Father and Mother of the Ineffable Name, or if further reduced we get 6, which is equivalent to V, the Son. IHV, it will be remembered, represent the three simple letters which, according to the Sepher Yetzirah, were chosen by God as His Name in the six Directions.

The total number of Sephiroth and Paths is 193 plus 582 = 775. This reduces to 10, and therefore to Unity.

But the Points of the 20 Kethers are so arranged as to form when connected, TWELVE perfectly regular Pentagons. Thus the whole structure indicates a perfect DODECAHEDRON[1] and, when enclosed in the circumscribing SPHERE, touches it at eighty points.

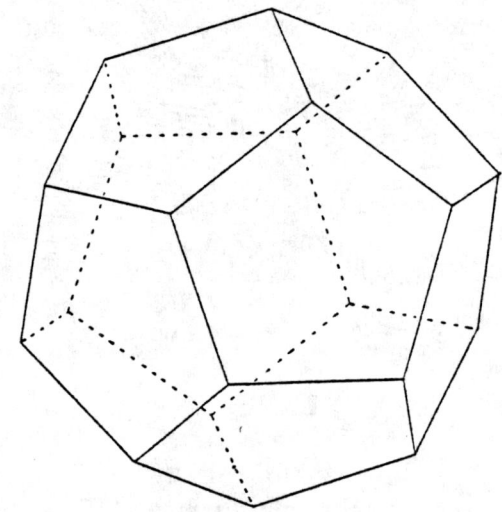

Figure XXXII

---

[1] See footnote to page 70.

Another confirmation comes from Dr. Karl von Eckhartshausen, Aufschlüsse zur Magie, Munich 1791, Vol. 4., Page 333. "As God contains All in the Spiritual, so does the Materia Prima, as typus, contain all in the Corporeal. The little parts of the Materia are pyramidical, triangular, tetera, dodecedra—always the image of the intellectual."

THE BODY OF GOD

The whole solid may be considered as capable of expansion by means of the progression of the unit "Trees" as explained before. Likewise, it is possible to imagine the reduction or contraction of the whole figure upon the Infinitely Small. (See Plate E.)

We have therefore discovered in the "Tree of Life," properly Multiplied and Projected according to the Art of the Wise, what may well be looked upon as the Anatomy of the Body of God, or the natural structure of Matter under the Influence of the Concealed Spirit. Thus the "Unknown Warrior" who made some such assertion in the presence of Frater Perdurabo, and earned such scant praise, may have been inspired to a degree he, himself, little realized.

The following quotation from "The Two Creation Stories" by James S. Forrester-Brown throws valuable light upon the conception of the Tree of Life as the Anatomy of the Body of God.

"When the Divine Will is born in the heart of a human soul, true free-will begins, for will is only free when in accord with the Great Will. Knowledge follows, and life becomes full of meaning and purposeful activity. The drama of the formal life (the tree of knowledge) develops in terms of the Higher Will (the tree of life), so that daily happenings appear to lift the veil from universal truths, illuminating the life. When the tree of knowledge and tree of life, reason and intuition, the personal and the universal, are harmoniously united in the individualized soul, the daily life becomes the moving image and expression of the living Soul of the universe.

"We may think of the tree of life as the arteries of the Great Cosmic Body. Through these arteries, as along channels, the cosmic Life pulses forth with every heart beat of the

Great Person. This is a very deep mystery. Until this Life is caught up by each individualized soul and returns through himself to the Great Cosmic Person, flowing back along the veins of the Great Body, there is no possibility of the power within the separated soul affecting the Great Person. Moreover, unless a counter-current is set up, the Life flows past the soul, and this does not truly live. The individualized soul requires to fashion capillaries throughout his nature and keep them in use, to allow of the return flow through them into the cosmic veins. That this shall be established he must, greatly daring, yet with awe and humility, seek to know the nature of God and of man and the relation between them. When he is able to see himself as he actually is, he realizes with a sense of abasement the imperfections and impurities of his complex personality, and the immediate necessity to turn from death unto Life. This does not imply a purely temporary repentance, but a Great Act of turning back, which cleanses the entire life of the soul and establishes organic relations with the Cosmic Person, making it possible for the "Christ" consciousness to be born "from Above" within the soul.

"The tree of knowledge is then seen as the veins of the Great Body along which flow back the counter-currents carrying the fruitage of the time-order, and thus the tree of life, with its arteries along which cosmic life is 'timelessly' propelled from the Great Heart, is complemented. The two trees 'in the midst of the garden' become united within the Cosmic Heart and Body, the 'Eden,' of the Great Person, and the 'Christ' consciousness is complete.

"The tree of life may also be thought of as the tree of universal life growing round and encompassing the individual soul. When that tree is truly one with the tree of phe-

THE BODY OF GOD 77

nomenal self, the tree of knowledge, then the abstract and the concrete, the ideal and the actual are one, and their fruits are living powers. From this universal-personal tree spring *all* the virtues, and on it they blossom and ripen. They are the fruits of temporal experience, containing the seeds of eternal Life, and, as such, correspond to the disciples of one's own 'Christ within' at the final Consummation.

"In the Apocryphal literature, Michael, Archangel of the Sun, is set over the tree which, at the time of the great judgment (note the position of "The Judgment" as Shin on the Tree. Achad.), is given over to the righteous, who obtain Life from its fruit. This is the tree of universal life, now one with the personal tree in the region of material existence."

CHAPTER IX

LET us now make a brief résumé of our work so as to keep in mind a clear conception of the various stages through which it has passed; but in order to show the progress that has been made in the solution of the Mysteries of the Holy Qabalah, we may look back a few years in order to see more clearly the results of the influence of the New Aeon and the rapid strides which have been made since its incoming in the year 1904 E. V.

In the year 1886, which happens to be that of the birth of the present writer, Dr. W. Wynn Westcott, Hon. Magus of the Soc. Ros. in Ang., translated the ancient treatise known as the "Sepher Yetzirah" into English, and read the results of his pioneer work before the Hermetic Society in London. In 1887 his work was published in a limited edition of 100 copies by Robt. H. Fryar of Bath, England.

Commenting upon Verses 9-10-11 of Chapter I, which have been quoted in full in Chapter VI of the present treatise and which described how IHU looked above and sealed the height, below and sealed the depth, etc., Dr. Westcott gives the following diagrams together with the words, "Note the description of the Decad. First a tetrad is formed, then a hexad." And that was all the explanation which seemed necessary, or was forthcoming, at the time. Not in any spirit of criticism, but, as stated above, in order to show the

THE BODY OF GOD

real progress which has been made, we should compare the simple diagram of the "hexad" with Plate B of the present work, and we can hardly fail to notice signs of genuine advance in Qabalistic thought during the last 37 years.

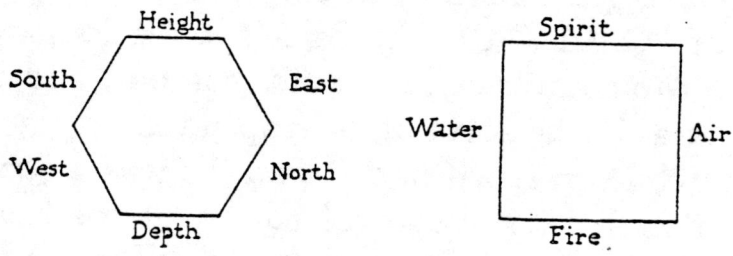

Figure XXXIII

From Dr. Wynn Westcott's Work.

But the ancient Sepher Yetzirah itself, although giving a possible indication of this six-fold development as being present in the mind of the writer, or compiler, in the distant past, contains little that could be construed as an indication of the further development of the Idea in *three-dimensional* form as suggested by the present author. There is a verse in Chapter II which reads: "These twenty-two letters, the foundations, He arranged as on a sphere, with two hundred and thirty-one modes of entrance. If the sphere be rotated forwards, good is implied, if in a retrograde manner, evil is intended," but it is doubtful if this can be thought to indicate the formation of the Dodecahedron and its infinite progression or expansion. Rather we are inclined to think we have taken a step not previously written of, or contemplated in any of the old treatises on the subject.

In May of last year (1922 E. V.), as the result of a series of Initiations of a very *direct nature*, dating particularly from June 21st, 1916, and developing on different Planes, December 21st, 1917, September to October,

1918, December 22nd, 1918, April, 1921, etc., the present writer obtained a clue to a new intellectual conception of the Qabalistic Plan. It seemed that although the 10 Sephiroth were in proper order and arrangement, the "Paths" could be changed to great advantage, and this resulted in the publication of "Q.B.L." or The Bride's Reception, which was an attempt to show clearly the old methods, and contained the new ideas in the form of an Appendix.

Meanwhile, in April of this year, he was led to discover a much more harmonious explanation of the Keys of the Tarot when they were arranged on the Tree according to the Revised Order of the Paths. The results of this investigation have been recorded in "The Egyptian Revival," to which I must refer the reader. I may say that this book seems an indication of the revival of the lost Universal Tradition of the Golden Age and explains the nature of the present Egyptian Revival in a reasonable manner.

This work led on to the discoveries recorded in the present treatise, which may be briefly summed up as follows:

The Tree of Life in its regular and simple form has been taken as the basis of our work, but the revised order of the Paths adopted, as the one which seems most reasonable.

It became apparent that the due proportions of the parts of the Tree had not previously been taken into serious consideration as of vital importance to the study of the matter. Examples of the designs of "Trees" in well known works on the subject, show great variation in this respect.

We discovered that the basis of the Tree was the Equilateral Triangle, the Vesica Piscis and the rectangle formed on its length and breadth. These were shown to have marvelous properties which have been sufficient to interest and impress some of the most learned and wise men of past his-

THE BODY OF GOD

tory, and upon which the style of Gothic Architecture is wholly based. But the fact that the Qabalistic "Tree of Life" in its entirety partook of these same marvelous properties, came to us as a new revelation.

We found that the "Tree" was not fixed, but capable of indefinite expansion or contraction, so that it truly *lived*, and that all our "Ideas" and "Correspondences" based thereon, were similarly capable of indefinite progress, thus enabling the mind of man to expand or contract at will, without interfering with its balanced and equilibrated arrangement once the Plan of the Tree had become firmly rooted therein.

We then discovered that, as indicated in the "Sepher Yetzirah," this plan could be multiplied when arranged as an ever-increasing Hexagon, based upon the progression of SIX TREES reflected in the Height, Depth, North, South, East and West. This we found to be the design of the naturally crystallized Snow-flake, and it gave us the means of filling all two-dimensional Space.

We further discovered that the Original Tree might be considered as a Prismatic Solid in Three Dimensions and that FIVE such prisms formed a perfect Pentagonal Figure when united. In other words the means of changing the Hexagram into the Pentagram is through a transition from 2 to 3 dimensions, as can be simply shown if we take a piece of paper, cut into a perfect Hexagon, or Hexagram, and then make another cut from one point to the centre, as in the following diagram.

We shall find that this piece of paper will fold into a perfect Pentagon or Pentagram if we slide one half of the divided point "A" under the figure till it coincides with "B," thus raising the centre of the figure into the third dimenson.

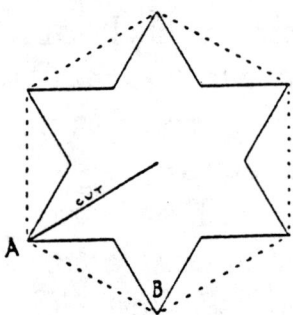

Figure XXXIV

Four of these blocks of Five Trees were found to form a solid capable of progression in all directions so as to fill every dimension of known space, and the nature of the whole figure was found to be that of a perfect Dodecahedron[1] or Twelve-fold figure, each side of which is a perfect Pentagon. Perhaps this represents the Tree in the Midst of the Garden[2] having Twelve manner of Fruits. Each of the surfaces being Pentagonal, represents a Microcosm or Type of Man and may be attributed to one of the Twelve Signs of the Zodiac, Twelve Tribes, Apostles, Knights of the Round Table, etc.

---

[1] Another reference from *The Secret Doctrine*, Vol. II, Page 39, may be of interest here. After mentioning the form of the Tree of Life, given in the Sacred Mysteries of the Mayas and Quiches, Madame Blavatsky continues: "This represents the same idea as the Sephirothal Tree, *ten* in all, yet when separated from the upper triad, leaving *seven*. These are the celestial fruit, the ten or one, ten born of *two invisible male and female seeds*, making up the 12, or the Dodecahedron of the Universe." This indicates that Madame Blavatsky had an idea that the Dodecahedron had some connection with the Qabalah, but evidently no comprehension of the solid prismatic sections, necessary for the building of this most perfect many-sided figure. She also remarks, Vol. II, page 485, "The Dodecahedron lies concealed in the perfect cube," say the Kabalists. I wish she had said which Kabalists; but the *cube* was always taken as the true Symbol of Matter and this obscure reference seems to indicate that if one understood matter, he would discover its structure to be that of the Dodecahedron. Achad.

[2] Our multiplied and progressed "Tree" may well be considered as the "Garden of Eden," but perfected in man's conception since all the "trees" are reflections of the One Tree of Life, the IDEA of which is concealed in the midst of the Garden.

THE BODY OF GOD

At the Centre of All is Malkuth, so that this is indeed the "Closed Palace of the Bride," the secrets of which were promised as a reward to those who succeeded in interpreting the Mysteries of the New Aeon.

This Prismatic and Crystalline conception of the "Tree" is perhaps the reward mentioned in Liber Legis of those who have passed the "Third Ordeal." Chapter III states:

"63. The fool readeth this Book of the Law and its comment: and he understandeth it not.

"64. Let him come through the first ordeal, and it will be to him as silver.

"65. Through the second, gold.

"66. Through the third, *stones of precious water*.

"67. Through the fourth, ultimate sparks of the intimate fire.

"68. Yet to all it shall seem beautiful. Its enemies who say not so, are mere liars.

"69. There is success."

But what of the ultimate sparks of the intimate fire? Who knows! There may be yet some further revelation before all is accomplished. But to my mind this refers to the Mystery of Hadit, the Concealed Centre, the Lost Father, Who is the Core of every Star, and the Flame that burns in every heart of man. For, since the the Universe is the Child of the Two Infinites, every point in space is equally the Centre of the Whole, and the Spirit of God is in each of us, as an ultimate spark of the intimate fire.

But, in any case, we have progressed, and we have discovered a strange new interpretation of the prophetic words of "Liber A'Ash," which states:

"This chain reaches from Eternity to Eternity, ever in triangles—is not my symbol a triangle?—ever in circles—

is not the symbol of the Beloved a circle? Therein is all progress base illusion, for every circle is alike and every triangle alike!

"But the progress is progress, and progress is rapture, constant, dazzling showers of light, waves of dew, flames of the hair of the Great Goddess, flowers of the roses that are about her neck, Amen!"

CHAPTER X[1]

AFTER this brief résumé we may once again turn our thoughts to the main results of our researches as summed up in the Dodecahedron within the perfect Sphere.

It would almost seem that our original Qabalistic conceptions have led us out of the realm of thought usually linked with the Hebrew Qabalah into an atmosphere of Intelligibles which is associated with the philosophy of the Masters in ancient Greece. Or, we may say, as our conceptions have expanded towards the Universal, we have contacted another set of teachings, thus uniting Hebrew and Greek thought.

Plato informs us in his *Republic:* "Geometry rightly treated is the knowledge of the Eternal," and he is reported by Plutarch to have said that "God is always geometrising." Nor was the conception of the Universe in the form of the Dodecahedron unknown to Plato, for in his *Timæus* this idea is clearly indicated.

But just *how* this solid figure was built up so as to symbolize the Universe in all its details, if known to the ancients, was not revealed. Let us see, however, what hints are to be found in the writings of other authorities.

Proclus, in his Introduction to Books II and III of Plato's *Republic,* says: "But the former (Vulcan) artifi-

---

[1] This Chapter and the one following were written in 1925, these references having come to my notice since I wrote the body of the book in 1923. Achad.

cially fabricated the whole sensible order, and filling it with physical reasons and powers. He also fashioned *twenty tripods* about the heavens, that he may adorn them with the most perfect of the many-sided figures and fabricates various and many-formed sublunary species." To which Thomas Taylor, the great Cambridge Platonist, adds, "Viz.: the dodecahedron, which is bounded by twelve equal and equilateral pentagons, and consists of twenty solid angles, of which the tripods of Vulcan are images; for every angle of the dodecahedron is formed from the junction of three lines."

There are several references to the dodecahedron in Madam Blavatsky's *Secret Doctrine,* among which the following is of special interest. "The most distinct and the one prevailing idea, found in all ancient teaching, with reference to Cosmic Evolution and the first 'creation' of our Globe with all its products, organic and *inorganic*—strange word for an Occultist to use!—is that the whole Kosmos has sprung from the Divine Thought. This Thought impregnates Matter, which is co-eternal with the One Reality; and all that lives and breathes evolves from the Emanations of the One Immutable Parabrahman-Mulaprakriti, the Eternal One-Root. The former of these, in its aspect of the Central Point turned inward, so to say, into regions quite inaccessible to human intellect is Absolute Abstraction; whereas, in its aspect as Mulaprakriti the Eternal Root of All, it gives one at least some hazy comprehension of the Mystery of Being.

"Therefore, it was taught in the *inner* temples that the visible Universe of Spirit and Matter is but the Concrete Image of the Ideal Abstraction; it was built on the Model of the First Divine Idea. Thus, our Universe existed from eternity in a latent state. The Soul animating this purely

THE BODY OF GOD

Spiritual Universe is the Central Sun, the highest Deity Itself. It was not the One who built the concrete form of the idea, but the First Begotten; and, as it was constructed on the geometrical figure of the *dodecahedron* the First Begotten 'was pleased to employ 12,000 years in its creation.'"

It would seem, from the above, that the "Model of the First Divine Idea" may have been very much in harmony with the ideal Formative Principle we have been studying.

This conception of the Universe as a Dodecahedron appears if not to have originated with Plato, to have first been mentioned by him in his writings. All the references I have so far discovered in connection with the idea, can be traced back to this source. Mr. Hartley Burr Alexander, of the University of Nebraska, makes some interesting remarks in this connection (Nature and Human Nature, P. 378). " 'We must conceive,' says Plato, 'of three natures: first, that which is in process of generation, and this would be the world of nature as we experience it; second, that in which the generation takes place, and this is the recipient or matrix of nature; and third, that of which the generated world is an image, and this is the cosmic reason or form. We may liken the receiving principle to a mother, and the source or spring to a father, and the intermediate nature to a child,' he says, and we think immediately of the mythopoetic union of Earth and Heaven and the Life of Nature which is its offspring. But for Plato this is a mere trope; he does not rest without being scientifically explicit. There are three kinds of being: that which is uncreated and indestructible, changeless, eternal, imperceptible to any sense, open only to the contemplation of the intelligence, and this is the principle of the Father, the ideal or formal essence of the world; again, that which is sensible and created and always in motion, the

Child, the world of change and life; and finally, there is a third nature, the Mother, which, like the Father, is eternal and admits not of destruction, which provides a home for all created things, and is apprehended 'without the help of sense, by a kind of spurious reason, and is indeed hardly real.' This nature is space, and we 'beholding as in a dream, say of all existence that it must of necessity be in some place and occupy a space, but that what is neither in heaven nor in earth has no existence.'

"This mothering space which is hardly real, yet is the cause of the determinism of nature, Plato identifies as the material element of being. As pure matter, it is purely indeterminate, but it is receptive of all determinations. The four elements, earth, air, fire and water, are formed from it, for 'the mother substance becomes earth and air, insofar as she receives the impressions of them.' Plato's conception of the formation of these elements from the original substance was as purely mathematical as are our modern physical notions. 'God fashioned them by form and number,' he says: and the forms which he assigned were the forms of the regular solids. Thus the form of the fiery element is the pyramid, of air, the octahedron; of water, the icosahedron; of earth, the cube. The fifth solid, the *Dodecahedron,* is the form of the universe as a whole, or perhaps one might say *the scaffold upon which the spherical universe is constructed.* Further, these elements are themselves compounded of simpler mathematical forms, the pyramid, octahedron and icosahedron of equilateral, the cube of isosceles triangles; so that if we regard the elements as molecules, we may view the triangles as atoms of the material substrate.

"Doubtless it was this geometrical account of matter which gave rise to the saying ascribed to Plato that 'God

THE BODY OF GOD

always geometrizes'—for God, says Plutarch in his commentary on the saying, made the world in no other way than by setting terms to infinite and chaotic matter."

There seems to have been many attempts to find a solution of this problem raised by Plato; and apparently as many failures. For instance, the author of "The Canon" remarks: "Nearly all the old philosophers devised an harmonic theory with respect to the universe, and the practice continued till the old mode of philosophizing died out.

"Kepler (1596), in order to demonstrate the Platonic doctrine, that the universe was formed of the five regular solids, proposed the following rule. 'The earth is a circle, the measurer of all. Round it describe a dodecahedron; the circle inclosing this will be Mars. Round Mars describe a tetrahedron; the sphere inclosing this will be Jupiter. Describe a cube round Jupiter; the sphere containing this will be Saturn. Now inscribe in the earth an icosohedron; the circle inscribed in it will be Venus. Inscribe an octohedron in Venus; the circle inscribed in it will be Mercury' ("Mysterium Cosmographicum," 1596).

"This rule cannot be taken seriously as a real statement of the proportions of the cosmos, for it bears no resemblance to the ratios published by Copernicus in the beginning of the sixteenth century. Yet Kepler was very proud of his formula, and said he valued it more than the Electorate of Saxony. It was also approved by those two eminent authorities, Tycho and Galileo, who evidently understood it. Kepler himself never gives the least hint of how his precious rule is to be interpreted."

The author of "The Canon" then submits a proposed plan of finding universal measurements symbolically concealed in the above rule, but in order to do this he assumes that the figures need not be taken as solids but as so many regular plane polygons. But this seems to me quite a departure from the problem. Also Plato connected these solids with the Elements rather than with the Planets.

But I think our complex solid will be found to contain those mentioned by Plato, although such a thought did not enter my mind until quite lately.

It should be remembered that the Qabalists attribute the four elements to Malkuth, which is often called the Sphere of the Elements. Now Malkuth has remained a perfect Sphere in our plan and in fact represents the Material Substance of the Universe. But the Qabalists have in particular attributed to Malkuth the Element of Earth, while to the next three Sephiroth, Yesod, Hod and Netzach, have been assigned Air, Water and Fire.

Earth, as Matter, has always been symbolized by the Cube, or the Cube within the Sphere, and we may well consider this Cube to be concealed in the Sphere of Malkuth.

The lower section of our Single Prismatic Tree, that representing the four lower Sephiroth of the Elements, is in the form of a perfect Tetrahedron, that is to say, a solid

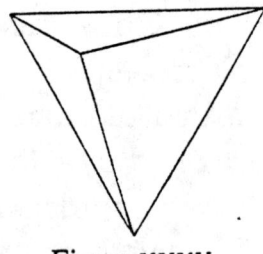

Figure XXXV

bounded by four plane triangular faces, each of which is equilateral. And again we find this same solid with a central core of Fire—the Path of Shin—comprising the com-

THE BODY OF GOD

binations of Chokmah, Binah and Tiphereth. Plato particularly attributes this form to Fire.

That portion of our Complete Complex Solid, representing the Elemental Sephiroth; viz., up to the Planes of "The Hierophant" which are penetrated by the Central Paths of Mem, or Water, is composed of twenty of the above solids so conjoined as to produce a perfect icosahedron, viz.: —a solid bounded by twenty equilateral triangles. This is particularly attributed to Water in the Platonic scheme.

When the progression is made to include Tiphereth, the twenty equilateral planes become points, or tripods which mark out the Dodecahedron, while the Second Progression of the Tree exactly encloses this. The points of the twenty Kethers indicate a similar but larger solid.

Thus we have disposed of four of the five regular solids.

The last, or octahedron, presents some difficulty. This is a solid bounded by eight equal and equilateral plane surfaces, and six summits or vertices. I have so far been unable to discover that such a solid exists within our complex solid while deriving its surfaces and angles from regular sections of the Tree.

But what at first sight appears a difficulty may possibly become a clue when we consider that this form is attributed to the Element of Air. Fire, Water and Earth are all perceptible to our sense of sight—not so Air. I do not want this to appear as an evasion of the issue, for in any case there are interesting indications of this missing form in the Tree of Life as originally outlined.

It will be found that four small equilateral triangles are shown on the Tree uniting the Six Sephiroth which are attributed to Vau in the Four-lettered Name, and Vau is the Letter of *Air*. These four triangles are arranged thus:

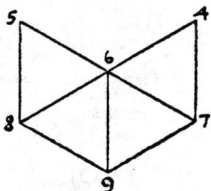

Figure XXXVI

It will be found that if a plane surface be folded on the lines where these triangles join, and if the points represented by Chesed and Geburah be drawn together, it forms exactly *one-half* of an Octahedron. And it may further be noted that, leaving out from the figure of the whole Tree that portion which represents our tetrahedron, plus Kether, the remainder has the following form:

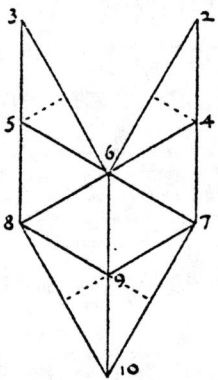

Figure XXXVII

This, it will be observed, represents the portion just described which makes up the half-octahedron, together with just enough additional surface material to form four other equilateral triangles required for the completion of the figure. But, without severing the fragments, we cannot take a sheet of paper and fold it into the desired shape, as was the case when making the solid prismatic Tree itself.

But even in the latter case a very interesting thing will

THE BODY OF GOD

be noticed—*the summit of the Supernal Triad disappears.* For, whether we take Three Trees connected at the side thus:

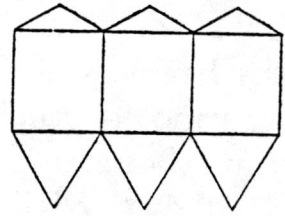

Figure XXXVIII

or Three Trees radiating from Kether thus:

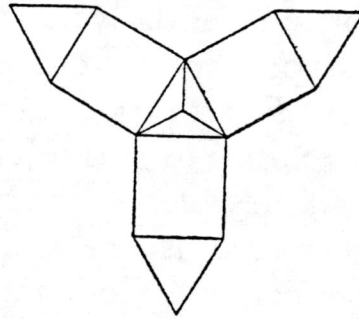

Figure XXXIX

we find, upon experiment in folding, that although the lower triangle fits together perfectly, when we bend the paper back along the lines of the Path of Aquarius we get a *flat top* with Kether on a level with Chokmah and Binah. Therefore, although for the sake of retaining the *appearance* of the original two-dimensional figure, we must build up a Summit to represent Kether; we do so, as it were, with apologies to The Supreme One which must ever remain *unmanifest* to our lower senses. In other words the Summit of the Supernals cannot be conceived as a "solid," or even as partaking of "form" in the realm of ideas. This, rather than detracting from our plan, leads us to a most important truth, viz.: that in our researches we must never for a moment forget the Superessential excellence of the ONE and the GOOD. For, as Simplicius beautifully observes, "It is requisite that he who ascends to the principle of things, should investigate whether it is possible there can be anything better than the supposed principle; and if something more excellent is found, the same inquiry should again be made respecting that, till we arrive at the highest conception, than which we have no longer any more venerable. Nor should we stop in our ascent till we find this to be the case. For there is no occasion to fear that our progression will be through an unsubstantial void, by conceiving something about the first principles which is greater than and surpasses their nature. *For it is not possible for our conceptions to take such a mighty leap as to equal, and much less to pass beyond the dignity of the first principle of things.*" He adds: "This, therefore, is one and the best extension (of the soul) to (the highest) God, and is as much as possible irreprehensible; viz., to know firmly, that by ascribing to him the most venerable excellencies we can conceive, and the most holy and primary names and things, we ascribe nothing to him which is suitable to his dignity. It is sufficient, however, to procure our pardon (for the attempt) that we can attribute to him nothing superior."

And in respect of our pardon we may devoutly hope that Simplicius was right.

THE BODY OF GOD

CHAPTER XI

LATO said in regard to the Elements of the Universe: "God fashioned them by form and number." We have had something to say about Form but have touched very little upon Number. It will be well for us to make a few observations in the light of the Forms we have reconstructed.

I shall have little to say in regard to the Numbers attributed to the ordinary Qabalistic Plan of the Sephiroth, these having been dealt with in "Q.B.L." and elsewhere. It is merely necessary to recapitulate as follows:

The simple two-dimensional figure consists of 10 Sephiroth; 10 being the sum of the numbers from 1 to 4. The importance of this lies in the Fourfold Nature of the Ineffable Name which is the Formula of the whole System. There are 22 (2 + 2 = 4) connecting links or Paths. These consist of 3 + 7 + 12, and correspond to the Elements, Planets and Signs of the Zodiac. In all we have 32, called, in relation to this System, the 32 Paths of Wisdom, representing the whole figure. One of the special virtues of this number is that it represents the coalescence of Macroprosopus and Microprosopus in the Divine Name AHIHVH, and thus shows the connection between Kether—The Highest Crown—and the Nine lower Sephiroth, which emanated from it.

When we allow this simple figure to expand in one direction, as previously explained, we find, since Malkuth remains One and the same throughout, that the Second Tree contains 19 Sephiroth. 19, which is a prime number, reduces by addition to 10. Likewise the Third Tree consists of 28 Sephiroth, a Perfect Number which again reduces to the original 10 and therefore to 1 or Unity. The Fourth Tree contains 37 Sephiroth, another prime number reducing to 10. The Fifth gives 46 which reduces to 10, while the Sixth represents 55 which not only does this but is the Sum of the Numbers from 1 to 10. And since the number of the Sephiroth will be increased by 9 at every progression, their total, at each step, will always reduce to 10 by addition.

The 22 Paths of the first figure will increase by 20's to 42, 62, and so on, since two of these—Beth and Daleth—retain their own nature indefinitely.

Thus the progressions of the whole Tree will be from the original 32 to 61 and so on; 29 being added each time.

We may now consider the outstanding features of the figure when shown expanding in Six directions as the Snowflake. Since Netzach and Hod now combine we have in all 49 Sephiroth in the unprogressed figure. This, it may be remarked, is a distinctly Venusian Number (that of the Intelligence of Venus) and the Square of Seven. It reduces to 13, the number of Unity and Love. The number of Paths in this figure is 126 (a number attributed to two important Names of God) and this, added to 49, gives 175 as the total number of Sephiroth and Paths. This, it may be remarked, is the Number of the Spirit of Venus. It represents the sum of the numbers from 1 to 49 divided by 7, and it again reduces by addition to 13.

THE BODY OF GOD

When we consider the progressions of this Sixfold Figure we find the Sephiroth increase by 48 each time, Malkuth remaining single. This is of interest because 48 is the numeration of KOKB, the Sphere of Mercury, and we find the particular feature of this Six-fold plan is that the Spheres of Venus and Mercury (Netzach and Hod) are forever united. I have always considered this word Kokab to be in some way connected with the words Khu and Khabs; Khu being the Magical entity of man, and Khabs meaning a Star. Considering this arrangement is as a Six-fold Star and the uniting of the Paths and Spheres of Venus and Mercury as Love under Will, this will be interesting to Students of the New Aeon.

The number of Sephiroth in the Second progression is therefore 49 + 48 = 97. This is another prime number and that of the Archangel of Netzach. It has many other correspondences, one of which is "An architect." The next progression gives us 145 which, according to the old arrangement, corresponds to the 13 Paths of the Beard of Microprosopus. But the Fourth progression produces 193, another prime number of particular importance since it is the Number of Sephiroth in the unprogressed but complete three-dimensional solid which forms the Dodecahedron. 193 also reduces to 13, which, it may be remarked, is the number of Sephiroth in the single prismatic solid.

The 126 Paths of the six-fold plan progress by adding 120 each time (since the Paths of Venus and Mercury are combined) and this is a very important Number to the Rosicrucian, and on account of its representing the God ON. Other interesting numbers can be traced out by the Student who possesses a copy of the *Sepher Sephiroth*. The whole figure progresses by the addition of 168 (the additional 48

Sephiroth and 120 Paths) and this is a very important Number, being that of the *Parentes Superni*.

We may now engage in a brief consideration of the Solid Figure. The first simple form contains 13 Sephiroth, which number gives it the Seal of Unity. This solid also contains 13 parts which produce the angles representing the Paths. Thus it represents 26, the Number of the Ineffable Name.

When this solid is extended in 20 directions (20 is the numeration of IvD the first letter of the Name spelt in full) 193 Sephiroth are produced. These added to the 260 (13 × 20) parts give 453, a number reducing to 12 which is the number of pentagonal faces on the 20-pointed dodecahedron. But, which is perhaps of greater interest, this number 453 is that of NPsh ChIH, the Animal Soul in its fulness; i.e., including the Creative Entity or Chiah. The importance of this will be plain when we remember that the total number of Sephiroth and Paths in the Whole Solid is—as has been shown in Chapter VIII—775 and this, added to the 260 parts or sectional solids, gives 1035 which is the sum of the numbers from 1 to 45. Now 45 being the numeration of ADM (Adam) indicates that we have once more shown the Qabalistic ADAM in all his Spiritual and Animal fulness and that he once again contains the sum of all his parts.

Also the 20 points and 12 faces of the dodecahedron equal 32, the original number of the Paths of Wisdom.

One other point seems worthy of notice in this connection. The *Sepher Yetzirah* makes a very strong feature of TEN Sephiroth (ten and not nine, ten and not eleven), and it may be assumed that we have departed entirely from this fundamental conception.

But it is also true that the ancient Qabalists considered

THE BODY OF GOD

the Three Veils of the Negative—A<small>IN</small>, A<small>IN</small> S<small>UPH</small>, A<small>IN</small> S<small>UPH</small> A<small>UR</small>—as depending back from Kether; thus, although these are *unmanifest*, the whole scheme was based on 13. It may be further remarked that there are Seven Sephiroth below the Supernal Triad and the Three unmanifest Ideas above, so that we have, as it were, $7 + 3 = 10$, $10 + 3 = 13$; the 10 standing midway between the 7 and the 13.

Now it has been pointed out that the progressions of the single Tree are made by the addition of nines, so that each number produced reduces to 10 when we add the digits. In this case, then, the essence of the original basis remains. Nor is this basis lost when we consider the Sixfold two-dimensional figure, the Single Prismatic solid, and the Twentyfold solid and their progressions, although it is more deeply concealed in these instances.

All these start from a basis of 13. The Single solid has 13 Sephiroth and increases by the addition of 12 at each progression. Thus the series is 13, 25, 37, 49, 61, 73, 85, etc. If we reduce these by addition (leaving the first as it stands) we obtain 13, 7, 10, 13, 7, 10, 13, etc. Now this is the series we noticed above in regard to the original Tree—the 10 Sephiroth with 3 Veils above the Supernal Triad and 7 Spheres below it. And this series recurs with every three progressions, so that since $7 + 10 + 13 = 30$, the *average* is still, in essence, 10 throughout.

And when we consider the Sixfold plan we start with 49 which reduces to 13, and progress by adding 48. Now 48 being 4 times 12 we find we are running in a series which coincides at certain definite points with the previous one, and the same peculiar rule is noticed in regard to our reductions of digits. Thus, 49, 97, 145, 193, 241, 289, 337, etc., etc., reduce to 13, 7, 10, 13, 7, 10, 13, etc., as before.

The same is true of the complete solid. We begin with 193 which reduces to 13, and progress by adding 192; which in this case is 4 times 48. Therefore we find the same underlying law if we consider 193, 285, 577, 769, 961, 1153, 1345, etc., with the exception of the one instance of 769 which reduces to 22 (the number of paths) on its way to its final reduction to 4 without first forming 13 as in all the other cases.

And we of course find that every fourth progression of one series coincides with the number produced by one of the others. Thus the fourth progression of the Prism gives us 49 which is the basic number of the Star. The fourth progression of the Star gives us 193, the basic number of the complete solid. The sixteenth progression of the Star gives us the fourth of the complete solid, and so on. In fact *every* progression of the Star will give a number which is that of some progression of the Simple Solid, and *every* progression of the Complex Solid a number equal to some progression of both the Star and the Simple Solid, and the numbers common to all will always reduce to 13 (or 4).

A word now in regard to the *proportion* of the various parts of our figures. We found in constructing the first simple plan of the Sephiroth and Paths that the proportion of the Diameter of the Sephiroth to the Width of the Paths was very important, especially in regard to the Progressions.

I noticed recently that in his footnotes to the new edition of Eliphas Lévi's Transcendental Magic, Mr. A. E. Waite makes the following remarks, evidently with the intention of discrediting Lévi: "In the Tree of Life KETHER, the Supreme Crown, abides above CHOKMAH and BINAH, forming with these the Supernal Triad, below which are CHESED and GEBURAH. It must be said further that the Tree comprises three triangles, beneath which is MALKUTH. There *is no*

THE BODY OF GOD

circle as Lévi suggests, except in the accidental sense that the names and titles of each Sephira are inscribed within this figure."

Without some idea of a Circle or Sphere, if only to represent the Absolute or the Universe, one can hardly conceive of any Qabalistic Scheme at all; and that all the Qabalists have merely used the Sephiroth as convenient receptacles for names and inscriptions while giving to the Paths any semblance of reality, seems to me rather puerile.

However, since the very Points representing the Centres of the Sephiroth in any properly proportioned "Tree" are produced by the original generating circles, we may leave aside Mr. Waite's remarks and consider the matter as if the Sephiroth were *Circles* and the Paths *Lines*.

In the construction of the Tree we commence with 4 generating circles. These may be of any desired size, but by their means we obtain the Centres of the Ten Sephiroth.

The logical diameter of each Sephiroth will be found to be one-fourth of that of the generating circles. This makes the length of the short Paths—such as Aleph—exactly equal to the diameter of each of the Sephiroth.

Next, in order to discover the logical *width* of the Paths we should examine the structure of the Tree where the five Paths from above unite in Tiphereth and the three proceed from below that Sphere. It will be noticed that the natural division of the circle will be into 12, as this will make all the Paths the same width and leave a space equal to the width of one path between the lower ones. Thus the width of each Path should be one-half the radius of the Sephira. (The greatest possible width without the Paths conflicting with one another above Tiphereth.)

When it comes to the progression of the Trees we shall then find that the *third* will produce Sephiroth equal in diameter to the original generating circles, while the width of the Paths of the *third* progression will be exactly that of the diameter of the Sephiroth of the first Tree.

A glance at the Coloured Plate will show how exactly all the details fit in if this plan is adopted; even in the case of the four-fold division of Malkuth the progressed Paths exactly coincide with the diagonals. (See Frontispiece.)

It should be remembered, however, that all our *measurements* are made from *centre* to *centre* of the Sephiroth.

As a further check on the correctness of the size of the Sephiroth we find that a Vesica constructed upon the Path from the centre of Chesed to that of Geburah, having a length from Kether to Yesod, will exactly touch the *circumferences* of Chokmah, Binah, Netzach and Hod.

Our final summary will deal with the *proportions* of the whole figure as based on those of the Vesica Piscis. We have shown the importance of 15 to 26 (the proportions of the Vesica) in relation to the sacred Names IH and IHVH. The Student may consider for himself such further proportions in this series as 30 to 52, 60 to 104, 120 to 208, 240 to 416. The last of these is of peculiar interest for 240 is NTZNIM, Prima Germina, and 416 is HRHVR, meaning Thought or Meditation. Again the next proportion, 480 to 932, is important. 480 is LILITH and 932 is OTZ HDOTH TVB VRO, The Tree of the Knowledge of Good and Evil. This is surely a valuable correspondence worthy of study.

But there is another set of proportions in connection with the Vesica, viz.: 30 to 52. 30 is the Letter of Libra—Balance; 52 is the numeration of ABA VAMA (Father and Mother), AIMA (The Supernal Mother—fertilised), and of

THE BODY OF GOD

BN (The Son: Assiah's "Secret Nature"). The correspondence between these and Balance is an interesting one.

Further we may use 52 to 90, with startling results, for 90 is SvD HvvG, The Mystery of Sex. This, as applied to ABA VAMA, AIMA, or BN leads to ideas suitable for the highest "meditation" about which we should be "very silent." (Strangely enough, as I wrote this I noticed another correspondence, for ZMH, Meditation, adds to 52, and DOMM, Very Silent, adds to 90. I shall therefore take this as a "hint" and pass on.)

The next proportion 90 to 156 is of even deeper significance for here we find the relation between "The Mystery of Sex" (90) and BABALON (156) The Victorious Queen. (Vide XXX *Aethyrs:* Liber CDXVIII).

And the very next progression 156 to 270 gives us a relation between BABALON (156) and I.N.R.I. (270). Enough has been said to indicate to the Adept that a study of these proportions is well worth while.

But, so far we have been dealing with the actual proportions of the Vesica, and we have not mentioned those of the complete Tree of Life itself. Those of the Vesica being as 26 to 45 we see the proportions of the tree must be 26 to 60, or, since we can divide by 2, we may put them at 13 to 30. Here we enter upon the consideration of our basic number 13 (Unity and Love) in right relation with "Balance." For "Equilibrium is the Basis of the Work."

We again obtain an interesting series of proportions, 13 to 30, 26 to 60, 52 to 120, 104 to 240, 208 to 480, 416 to 960, etc., but these will again be left to the consideration of the Student for we have yet to deal with a greater Mystery.

If 13 to 30 is the exact width and height of the two-dimensional figure of The Tree of Life, what will be the proportions that will give us the correct angle of the Supernal Triad in order to change this to a Solid? The present angle is 120 Deg., the interior angle of the Hexagon; what proportion will give us the interior angle of the Solid Pentagon by which Kether, Chokmah and Binah take their places each touching the circumscribing SPHERE?

This final revelation, only made to us on May 30th, 1925, yet necessary to the completion of our treatise, has come as the Seal of the Supreme upon our Work. It is not possible to enter into the proper consideration of the importance of this discovery in relation to the Magical life-work of the Author and to the Mysteries of the New Aeon.[1] For the present, therefore, we simply state this proportion to be as THIRTEEN is to THIRTY-ONE.

13 to 31 gives the exact angle of 108 degrees necessary to the building up of our solid, the additional part being used to raise the Point of Kether to the Pinnacle of the Solid.

But let us examine the progressions of this proportion as before. We obtain: 13 to 31, 26 to 62, 52 to 124, 104 to 248 and 248 to 496. This last, be it noted, is the *Fifth* progression.

Now let us remember that the *Fifth* Progression of Malkuth as an expanding Sphere is the one which First embraces the Kether of the First Tree (and the Dodecahedron formed by the Tiphereths of the Second Tree). How many Sephiroth shall we find in the Complete Solid at the Fifth Progression? $193 + 192 + 192 + 192 + 192 = 961$. Therefore when the Sephiroth have increased to 961 in the Solid, *Malkuth* will have expanded to the First Kether.

---

[1] These matters will be dealt with in "The Alpha and Omega of Initiation" to be published later.

THE BODY OF GOD

961 *happens* to be 31 × 31, or the Square of 31, and it reduces to 13.

But what of our *Proportion* of 208 to 496, the *Fifth* progression of the proportions of 13 to 31? Not only is 208, the *width* of our Tree, equal to the *length* of a Pure Vesica whose breadth is 120 (our original Kether angle), but our other proportion 496 is a *Perfect* Number, the *Sum of the Numbers from One to Thirty-one*, and the *Numeration* of MLKVTH—Malkuth.

AL, it must be remembered, is the Highest Kether Name of God—31—which being read in reverse is LA, Not, and thus forms the true formula of the transition from the unmanifest to the manifest.

Let us never forget that the True Kether—Hadit—is forever *concealed* in the Centre of Malkuth, and that of this it has been written in Liber Al.vel Legis: I am NOT (La = 31) extended (1+2+3 . . . 31 = 496) and Khabs (a Star) is the Name of my House.

In concluding this section we may remark that the 76th progression of the Single Solid, and the 19th progression of the Star, show 913 Sephiroth. 913 is BRAShITH, Berashith. "In the Beginning"—the First Word of Genesis. The 80th progression of the Single Solid, the 20th of the Star, and the 5th of the Complete Solid, all give 961 (31×31), and in case you should forget this, all you have to do is to stand in The Kingdom, Malkuth (496), and LOOK UP. You will then see Yesod (9), and above that Tiphereth (6) and—by the Grace of God—Kether (1). So mote it be.

CHAPTER XII

UR intention was not that this should be a long treatise, but rather to give the gist of our discoveries to the world, thus allowing the inexhaustible treasures of this System to be mined and used by any who desire to grasp the opportunity.

But this work would not be complete unless we had a few words to say upon the possibilities of using this Plan as a basis upon which to build a new and more glorious Temple than has been conceived in the past, by the mind of Man.

My first appeal is therefore made to all Architects, and it is made in the Name of the Great Architect of the Universe, the Designs of Whose Trestle-Board, we cannot but feel, have been transmitted to us in such a marvelous manner.

The author feels that this represents the revelation of the "Formative Plane" of the Holy Qabalah, which contains the Influence of the "Archetypal" and "Creative" Worlds, and through which the Material Universe came into manifestation.

The discoveries in regard to the marvelous properties of the "Vesica Piscis" and the "Trinity in Unity" so much influenced the minds of Men in the Middle Ages, that a vast number of beautiful Gothic Cathedrals were planned and built with every detail lovingly worked out so as to symbolize the highest religious truths then open to the minds

THE BODY OF GOD

of men, in a material form. These Gothic structures are certainly admitted to be the most beautiful in design, but to some extent the secret of their proportions has been lost. The Spirit behind such buildings has been overlooked, and modern Architects have not had the same urge and impulse towards planning such perfect work.

But even in Gothic Churches, the symbolism of the Ground Plans was comparatively narrow in conception, and principally based on the Christian ideas of the Cross, although of course the Cross has a wonderful Natural Symbolism which is far older than what we term Christianity.

But never before, perhaps, in the History of Mankind, has it been so necessary that a Universal Temple be built; never before, perhaps, have the Plans been available.

When we realize that the "Tree of Life" not only partakes of all the properties of the "Vesica Piscis" but in addition to symbolizing the Mysteries of the Trinity, is capable of forming a Symbolic Basis for every Idea in the Universe, Natural, Human and Divine (as a slight study of the Qabalistic System will prove to any intelligent person); what a wonderful Ground Plan does it make for a Universal Temple, when we consider the possibilities of its indefinite Multiplication as a Six-fold Star, its Prismatic Proportions, etc. This should be sufficient to fire the minds of the World's Greatest Architects with enthusiasm to work out Designs for the First Great Temple built directly upon the Natural Formative Plans of the Grand Architect of the Universe. In such a Temple all Nations and Peoples might well meet to give praise to the One Whose Absolute Wisdom and Supreme Intelligence has built this Universe, and made it possible for created Man to comprehend its hidden Designs and to become a conscious co-operator in the Divine Plan.

My next appeal is to those in temporal charge of the Spiritual welfare of Mankind; the Heads of the various Religions of the World, those who claim to hold the Divine Authority for the instruction of Humanity and have charge of the welfare of their souls.

A Universal Teaching is needed, based upon simple and intelligible lines. A teaching that at once conforms with true Science and with the Universal experience of Humanity. Hitherto, the Great Teachers and founders of Religions have come to certain nations, or countries, and have taught a suitable doctrine for the particular climate and people to which their Mission led them. No public universal teaching has hitherto been possible on account of the lack of proper means of communication. Today we have the means of flashing the truth to every part of the globe in a few minutes. There is no longer any reason why a Universal Teaching should not be obtained and given to all humanity. Such an ideal condition cannot be brought about while there is contention and schism and conflicting basic ideas within the Churches themselves. I do not say that all humanity should be taught exactly alike, but I do say that there is but One Truth, and that One Truth is back of every exterior organization, however differently it may be interpreted.

Symbolically, at least, our present plan proves itself to be the basis of the Catholic Mysteries; it is undoubtedly the basis of the lost Jewish Tradition, which itself came from Egypt. It is the basis of Pythagorean Philosophy, of Geometry; it is the basis of the Rosicrucian Mysteries, as well as of Masonry, and will prove itself to be the Key to the Mysteries of the Secret Schools.

There is no reason why a Temple built on such perfect symbolism should not be equally sacred to Jewish, Catholic,

THE BODY OF GOD

Masonic and other Religious and Philosophical divisions of Humanity, wherein each could behold the Mysteries of their Tradition and realize that they are of the same Divine Origin. Scientifically, since every drop of water naturally crystallizes in this way, and Crystals are built up on similar lines, even the Materialist must recognize the Work of the Creator, as symbolized in such a structure.

My next appeal is to those in whose charge is the Civil destiny of the Nations. How can any peace of a lasting nature be brought about unless some Universal Plan is adopted in which every Nation will be seen to have its definite function, and have a well defined destiny? An understanding of the fundamental working principles of the Universe, and of the Working Plans of the Great Architect, is essential to a clear vision of what is needed to overcome the present difficulties with which mankind is confronted on every side. Things must be looked at from the point of view of the Whole, rather than that of the Part, if a proper Order and Arrangement is to be brought about. Man has been given free-will, which includes the possibility of making mistakes. Man is responsible for the welfare of this Planet, and those in authority have the responsibility on their shoulders of making this Earth a Heaven or a Hell for their brothers and sisters. Those in such positions cannot shirk this responsibility, and they cannot expect to be long in power if they wilfully neglect to *train themselves* to hold their office rightly and for the good of those in their charge.

Let them remember that the essence of Order consists in the perfect adjustment of all the parts in subservience to the Whole; and that, conversely, it is fatal folly to try to make the Whole conform to the design of some distorted part.

Civilization has been a failure, with all its apparent improvements and facilities, through failure to understand this general principle. It is absolutely essential that each part should discover its true function in relation to every other part, and to the Whole, and then fulfill its destiny without making any attempt to interfere with the proper functioning of the other parts of the Great Machine.

Equilibrium is the basis of the work. Every apparent pair of opposites can be reconciled in a third idea from which they both spring, and which contains the essence of both.

My next appeal is to all Thinking people. Many of you are slaves to your own thought. You are limited by your own narrow conceptions, which must always be narrow compared to the Infinite. Most of you know a lot of things that are not so in reality. To you I make this appeal. Clean out your minds, learn to control thought. Arrange your ideas in proper balanced order, and make your viewpoint one of equilibrium. Base your mental structure on the "Tree of Life" and since every idea placed thereon is capable of infinite progress, your minds will expand to the comprehension of all that is within Time and Space, for the Spirit of God in Man is capable of extending the Substance of every Mind which does not exert all its efforts to narrow the limits of consciousness to conform to a few personal prejudices and petty ideas. Why accept *less than is your due;* restriction is the only sin.

Lastly, I greet the Crowned Children of the New Aeon, those who, having sworn to overcome all things, shall obtain the reward promised to everyone that overcometh. And I say unto you, as One did of old: "In my Father's House are many Mansions, and if it were not so I would have told you." But also I add: There is a place prepared for every

THE BODY OF GOD

one of you, Here and Now. There is a place for everything, when all things shall be put in place. Take up your places in the Kingdom of the Ever-Coming Son, fulfill yourselves, in the fulfillment of the Will of God within you, and show those who are still in darkness without, that there is room for all who are prepared to keep their place, and cease from trying to usurp that of others. For:

Love is the law, love under will,

and through Love alone may ye come to the knowledge of the One Substance, capable of Infinite Multiplication and Projection, whereby ye become actual communicants in the Body of God.

In the Name of the One, by the Grace of God Triune, and by the Favour of the Ever-Coming Son,

AUMN

①

⑥

⑨

㊍